WHAT EXCELLENT
COMMUNITY COLLEGES DO

WHAT EXCELLENT COMMUNITY COLLEGES DO

Preparing All Students for Success

Joshua S. Wyner

Harvard Education Press
Cambridge, Massachusetts

Library of Congress Control Number 2013951059

Paperback ISBN 978-1-61250-649-4
Library Edition ISBN 978-1-61250-650-0

Published by Harvard Education Press,
an imprint of the Harvard Education Publishing Group

Harvard Education Press
8 Story Street
Cambridge, MA 02138

Cover Design: Steven Pisano
Cover Photo: Christopher Futcher/E+/Getty Images
The typefaces used in this book are Adobe Garamond Pro and Scala Sans.

This book is dedicated to people—in and out of community colleges—
who commit their days to bettering the lives of others; to my beloved wife,
Beth Parkinson-Wyner, who shows me what that looks like every day;
and to our wonderful children, Jack and Miles.

CONTENTS

FOREWORD

COMMUNITY COLLEGES TODAY OCCUPY A pivotal role in our country's educational system. From their modest roots as extensions of public high schools more than a century ago, designed in large measure to prepare elementary school teachers and offer a mix of liberal arts and vocational training, community colleges since 1901 have served more than 100 million people. Currently there are some twelve hundred community colleges—or sixteen hundred, when all branch campuses are included—and they educate almost half of the nation's undergraduates. All told, they represent an educational marketplace of remarkable diversity and choice.

In *What Excellent Community Colleges Do*, Joshua Wyner profiles the exemplary colleges that were selected as finalists for the Aspen Prize for Community College Excellence in 2011 and 2013 based on their performance in four essential areas: completion, equity, learning, and labor market outcomes. These widely varied schools—some are highly urban with a large minority population, others are rural and mostly white, and still others are mixed—provide a snapshot of a sector that is undergoing rapid and overdue change in its most fundamental structures, goals, and measures of success.

The very success of community colleges has placed them under unprecedented pressure. Community colleges are already complex networks with multiple performance standards. The result, increasingly, is that community colleges are at the forefront in the transformation of higher education from a mission somewhat vaguely defined by the general pursuit of knowledge to a more complex set of missions governed by overlapping but separable outcomes. The challenge going forward is to make the matrix of missions and outcome standards explicit.

Two of the community college missions are primary. The community college has emerged as the primary "on-ramp" to a bachelor's degree as well as the "off-ramp" to a job; it is the interface not only between high school and a four-year college, but also between would-be workers and employers. The modern community college is the gateway for poor, minority, and immigrant students who seek to realize the American Dream. Community colleges are filled—and frequently overrun—with high school students taking college-level courses prior to graduation, high school graduates taking remedial courses before they can embark on standard college-level courses, and full- or part-time students taking courses to fulfill a range of ambitions, from short-term job training to a four-year college degree. For many, arguably most, of those students, a certificate with immediate labor market value, an associate's degree, or a bachelor's degree is the must-have prerequisite to a decent-paying job.

Amid all this, community colleges—like the rest of higher education—are facing demands to help improve on national outcomes that are often lackluster when compared to our country's performance twenty-five years ago as well as to current global competition. A generation ago, the United States led the world in the number of postsecondary graduates; today it ranks in the middle tiers of the most advanced nations and is gradually being overtaken by rapidly developing and more populous countries, notably China and India.

Given the rising expectations, it was inevitable that the format of the community college, as we have known it for decades, would be compelled to change. And, in fact, the higher education system is being subjected to the same market forces that have already revolutionized big business and are starting to make significant inroads in the health-care industry.

THE BUSINESS OF COMMUNITY COLLEGES: PAST, PRESENT, AND FUTURE

For many decades, community colleges operated much the same way other colleges did—with relative freedom from government oversight and with the autonomy to determine what programs and delivery models were best for their consumers. Not surprisingly, they followed the efficient industrial organizational model of the twentieth century: a top-down hierarchy organized to deliver standardized goods or services. Competition within this model—for business and for higher education—meant reaching ever more consumers with a standardized product at lowest cost. For community colleges, success in delivering the core product was defined, well into the 1980s, primarily as increasing higher education access.

But expanding access translated into a steady shift in the nature of the community college consumer over time. The passage of the GI Bill in 1944 opened college doors to a multitude of students, followed by a huge enrollment of baby boomers in the 1960s. In more recent years, expansion has ushered in large numbers of low-income, minority, and adult students who bring with them a set of expectations and challenges very different from those of the traditional twentieth-century college student. Community colleges now serve a disproportionately large percentage of the nation's low-income and underrepresented minority students.

In addition to the complexities of a shifting consumer base, ever-expanding access has been increasingly in tension with the ever-expanding variety of missions and purposes served by the community college sector. The top-down model was enormously successful at delivering mass-produced goods and services, including mass education. It is less well designed for providing individualized educational programs across a multitude of vocational and academic programs to highly diverse students. In community colleges, as in any business, this fragmentation makes performance measurement and cost control equally challenging. It is difficult to bring quality and innovation to scale in fragmented systems, and the fragmented industry that is community colleges had fallen behind other industries in mobilizing capital for investment in technology—the investment that industries have most often utilized to move their production models into the twenty-first century.

Indeed, despite these changes in both the consumer base and the diversity of programs community colleges offer, the fundamental business model of the sector has remained unchanged. Consequently, the fragmented service delivery of community college education has provided variety, but has not been able to provide a large set of outcomes with consistent quality, or even to establish coherent outcome measures as singular drivers of organizational improvement. Put another way, community colleges are marvelous at pursuing many different missions but rarely excel in any of them. While manufacturing and many service industries underwent sweeping transformations as they moved from top-down hierarchies to network systems, the institutional transformation in higher education, from fragmented delivery systems to coherent networks driven by outcome standards, is still a relatively new idea. For example, the shift from accreditation based on inputs toward a more outcomes-driven system is barely under way in higher education.

If the transition in other goods and service industries is any guide, technology will play a major part in the transformation of the education system. Information technology has the potential to fundamentally reinvent higher education, just as it has car manufacturing, insurance, and government services. After all, higher education is at its core a business designed around the transfer of information, so the educational system ought to be particularly susceptible to the applications of information technology.

We have yet to see whether community colleges—and higher education more broadly—can reorganize themselves to take advantage of technological innovations in order to bring about sustained improvements in quality *and* productivity. While online study has been around for a few decades, the pace of its adoption is rapidly accelerating, at both for-profit and nonprofit institutions. One survey in 2010 found that enrollment in online education grew by 21 percent in the previous year, compared with 2 percent in higher education overall; more than 5.6 million, or nearly one-third of all students, were taking at least one course online in 2010, and one can only assume that number has risen substantially since then with the continuing economic slowdown and the proliferation of MOOCs (massive open online courses).

The larger question, however, is whether and how community colleges will meet the demands placed upon them by the twenty-first-century economy. Through 2020 the U.S. economy will create some 24 million new (not including replacement) job openings, at least 65 percent of which will require applicants to have some form of postsecondary education.[1] The fastest-growing and most lucrative of these jobs—in STEM, health care, and community and social services—are also those that will require the highest levels of postsecondary education. Based on current output, the labor market will want for nearly 5 million college-educated workers just in numbers alone. And the skills those college-educated workers bring may also be lacking: employers will increasingly look for high-level thinking and communication skills rather than just the physical skills associated with industrial-era manufacturing jobs. Community colleges must be central to the development of this educated work force, but their success in doing so will require not only changing the way they do business in order to make sure more students graduate or transfer, but also integrating technology, twenty-first-century skills, and real-world learning into their delivery and pedagogical models.

MAKING STUDENT SUCCESS THE BUSINESS OF COMMUNITY COLLEGES

The community college sector is in a state of flux as it adapts to rapidly increasing institutional performance requirements and a fast-changing student body. In some respects, community colleges are the poster children of change within complex environments. They have, in general, always been more adaptive to changing social conditions than more traditional four-year colleges, where the in-residence chalk-and-talk model of education still dominates. And yet the fundamental structures of community colleges have not evolved to make *student success the core business*—regardless of mission or niche.

Community colleges have always had multiple missions. They are traditional educational institutions embodying the belief that the purpose of higher education is to enhance individuals' lives and intellects, and thus they offer general liberal arts foundations meant as springboards to four-year institutions. At the same time, they serve as bridges into employment, recognizing that it is hard to participate fully in a market economy without real, marketable skills. As organizations, however, community colleges still often struggle to define a set of measurable, meaningful outcomes around which to organize their human and physical resources, their production models, or their investments in new technologies. It is hard to aim for a moving target, and community colleges still largely miss the mark.

Nonetheless, in *What Excellent Community Colleges Do*, Joshua Wyner provides a foundation for optimism. The community colleges featured in this book are almost a decade into a significant reform movement aimed toward sorting out missions and measurable outcome standards. They are exceptional not only for the outcomes they have achieved for their students—which is, let's be clear, the most important measure of success—but also because these institutions have achieved these reforms and practices absent the kinds of widespread incentives and shifts that drive change in industry. Where businesses have profit motives, definable shareholders, and at least somewhat predictable market conditions, community colleges rely on increasingly uncertain resources in the context of a multitude of public and private stakeholders, each with its own demands and competing visions for the "goods" public community colleges are expected to provide.

Too often in higher education research we start from the intervention and attempt to estimate its impact. We endorse best practices based on estimates that each has contributed in some statistically significant way to outcomes without having a clear definition of the end we hope to achieve through our innovations and interventions. Or we look at the challenges of higher education as isolated scholarly and practical challenges: developmental education, distance education, cost, completion. *What Excellent Community Colleges Do* does something different: it begins at the end, offering a pragmatic and holistic new vision of what excellence looks like at community colleges. It then illustrates practices and policies—some blatantly simple and others quite ingenious—that emerged as factors in the Prize finalist colleges' institution-wide approaches to ensuring success in learning, completion, and labor market outcomes for all of their diverse students.

Perhaps the book's most important contribution to the field at this moment is its analysis and understanding of the organizational cultures and structures of highly effective community colleges—colleges that have managed to make student success *their business* regardless of how their programs have evolved over time. Through the voices of dedicated practitioners at these exceptional colleges and explication of their practices, the examples presented here outline the shapes of an aspirational model for reform.

There is much yet to be done to make community colleges responsive to and successful in the twenty-first-century economy. But, given that so much of our country's future rests—and will increasingly rely—on community colleges, it is critical that we find ways to help them unlock their potential. *What Excellent Community Colleges Do* points us in that direction.

—Anthony P. Carnevale
Research Professor and Director
The Georgetown University Center
on Education and the Workforce

Introduction

COMMUNITY COLLEGES

A Call to Progress

O UR COUNTRY HAS AWAKENED TO the importance of community colleges. They educate 4 percent of the entire U.S. population—13 million students—each year. Most of the country's college freshmen and sophomores are in community colleges, whose relatively inexpensive tuition makes them a boon for Americans seeking a brighter future on constricted budgets. More than any other set of institutions, the nation's nearly twelve hundred community colleges are well positioned to meet the increasing demand for skilled workers in manufacturing, technology, health care, and other high-growth fields. They are a necessity for a nation trying, in an age of austerity, to reverse a steady decline in higher education attainment relative to the rest of the world.

But they don't always deliver on that promise. While access has expanded over the years, outcomes for students have not necessarily improved. So a new reform movement is taking hold, and community colleges are being pushed to achieve better results. Following repeated calls for improved graduation rates from national foundations, the Obama administration, and state governments, in 2012 the sector's own champion, the American

Association of Community Colleges, called student success rates "unacceptably low" and career training "inadequately connected to job market needs."[1]

Simultaneous recognition of community colleges' importance *and* poor student outcomes translates into enormous pressure. State funding is increasingly being tied to graduation rates (rather than to the number of students enrolled, the traditional method).[2] Federal and state agencies are requiring more public reporting on completion and employment outcomes. And for-profit competitors—investing in technology-based instructional delivery and using private-sector marketing techniques—are enrolling more and more students, including the low-income and minority populations long served by community colleges.

To attract students and public dollars in an era of accountability, transparency, and competition, community colleges must deliver significantly more degrees of higher quality at a lower per-pupil cost to an increasingly diverse student population—an equation that adds up to an immense challenge. In the balance is not just the colleges' survival but also continued opportunity for Americans—particularly the less advantaged—to access the knowledge and skills they need to have a secure future and to fuel our nation's economic growth.

But improvement is not coming easily, or quickly. Almost a decade into a new reform movement, there is not yet complete agreement about what community colleges should aim for, let alone good systems for measuring whether those goals are being attained. And there is not yet even universal acceptance of what, to most reformers, is a vital premise: it doesn't matter how many students enter community colleges' doors unless they exit with a meaningful credential in hand.

We are moving in that direction, however. With few exceptions, improving the rates at which students earn degrees and certificates lies at the center of recent change strategies, from state policy reform to financial aid redesign to efforts by state systems and nonprofit organizations to improve institutional practice. Completion matters to students; holding a degree or certificate is strongly correlated with having a good job with decent wages. Any significant attention to completion, then, is a dramatic improvement over the days when community colleges responded to ever-increasing enrollment numbers by developing more and more programs and courses, paying too little attention to whether students were succeeding in them.

As institutions and policy makers aim to improve community college completion rates, though, they must not do so at the expense of access. It's easy to increase the graduation rate if you just stop admitting the students least likely to succeed, if you invent policies and practices that effectively close doors to the rapidly growing numbers of minority and low-income young people who want to enroll—groups that historically have more trouble finishing college. And while nobody's recommending that as a remedy, it must be guarded against as a possible unintended consequence of the drive to improve completion rates.

But even maintaining access and improving graduation are not sufficient. After all, students don't go to community college to graduate; most go to acquire skills relevant to the careers they will pursue either directly out of community college or by way of a four-year school. Just as institutions work to increase the numbers of students who complete, they must put equal effort into ensuring the quality of their offerings and their instruction so that students leave well equipped to succeed in whatever comes next.

Facing a steady drumbeat to improve student outcomes, community colleges across the country are seeking more guidance on how to meet higher expectations. Already, a group of talented community college researchers, practitioners, and advocates has emerged. Some devote themselves to devising and testing the effectiveness of specific practices to increase success: learning communities that connect small groups of students across several classes, early warning systems to give struggling students the help they need, additional financial aid for students who achieve certain milestones, mandatory courses in study skills and career planning. Others are taking a more systemic approach, seeking to change state and federal policy or improve community college practice at multiple institutions at the same time.

Nearly all of these strategies aim primarily to increase the number of students who complete, and evidence suggests that they work only some of the time.[3] Indeed, community college graduation rates have not significantly increased over the past decade.[4]

This book seeks to contribute to the growing body of knowledge regarding how to increase community college student success, and thus help institutional leaders and policy makers understand important strategies for improving degree completion, equity, learning, and post-graduation outcomes. It draws on examples of what is happening at exceptional community colleges that were named finalists for the Aspen Prize for Community College Excellence over its first two years, as well as on understanding gained through the extensive data-gathering and selection process that begins with consideration of over one thousand community colleges each year. Profiles of the seven colleges that received the Aspen Prize's highest recognition and are highlighted in this book can be found in appendix A.

The Aspen Prize is built on a four-part definition of critical community college outcomes:

- *Completion.* Do students earn associate's degrees and other meaningful credentials while in community college, and bachelor's degrees if they transfer?
- *Equity.* Do colleges work to ensure equitable outcomes for minority and low-income students, and others often underserved?
- *Learning.* Do colleges set expectations for what students should learn, measure whether they are doing so, and use that information to improve?
- *Labor market.* Do graduates get well-paying jobs?

Pursuing and making significant progress on all of these goals is how exceptional community colleges ensure that diverse populations of students get what they came for: the knowledge and skills that will afford them a better life than they would have had otherwise. Achieving any one of these goals is better than improving access alone. Achieving all of them means a high-quality education for students, and a much brighter future for our country (see figure 1).

By starting with a holistic definition of excellence, measuring success against that definition, and then identifying practices and policies that align to high levels of student success, the Aspen Prize aims to help college leaders, educators, and policy makers better understand practices and policies that improve student outcomes *across entire institutions* as well as ones that may impede those efforts.

This book sets forth what's been learned about exceptional community colleges, especially from the schools recognized during the

FIGURE 1

Aspen Prize for Community College Excellence, indicators of community college excellence

WHY THIS MATTERS

Completion
Do students earn associate's degrees and other meaningful credentials, and bachelor's degrees after they transfer?

- Community college completion/transfer rates are under 40%.
- Completion of a credential leads to better employment and wage prospects.
- Completion data enables colleges to set goals and others to compare colleges.

Learning
Do community colleges set expectations for what students should learn, measure whether they are doing so, and use that information to improve?

- There is strong evidence that college rigor has diminished.
- Teaching students so they learn and develop skills is the core business of colleges, so this must be assessed.
- Professors cannot improve instruction without good information about what's working and what's not in their classrooms.

Labor market outcomes
Do students find long-term employment after graduation and earn a living wage?

- To prepare a skilled work force, colleges need to understand whether their programs are aligned with labor market needs.
- Students' post-graduation outcomes tell colleges whether their programs are succeeding and improving.
- Students should be able to choose a college and program knowing whether they'll be rewarded for their investment.

Equity
Do colleges work to ensure equitable outcomes for minority and low-income students, and others often underserved?

- Minority college students have historically succeeded at lower rates than others, yet can be successful with added supports.
- Increasing success for minority and low-income students is necessary to meet the country's growing need for better-trained workers.
- Expanding access and success helps fulfill the ideal of equal opportunity.

first year of the Aspen Prize.[5] Over the past two years, the Aspen Institute has engaged national experts in higher education research, practice, policy, and leadership to help figure out how to compare such varied institutions through the collection of qualitative and quantitative information. At the end of each analytic cycle is a $1 million prize, which, together with the promise of substantial publicity for the finalists and winners, has led to very high levels of participation.[6]

National data sets have limitations, so the Aspen Institute gathers information from multiple sources (see appendix B). In addition, the prize process takes into account the very different contexts in which community colleges operate and the many related variables, including student demographics, program offerings, regional economies, and state policies. The top-performing colleges in the prize competition vary significantly in demographics and program focus, showing that community college excellence comes in many packages (see figure 2).

Investigating and comparing quantitative and qualitative results at such diverse institutions requires accepting some measure of ambiguity. Among the greatest challenges are comparing completion rates at large urban and small rural colleges, or those at schools that award primarily career and technical credentials as opposed to those preparing most students for four-year transfer. In the face of such challenges, some resist the idea of transparently comparing community colleges based on imperfect measures.

But how else can we identify those exceptional colleges that are, systematically, doing the hard and smart work needed to achieve measurably high and improving levels of student success? The data available for analyzing institutional success—as opposed to

FIGURE 2

Aspen Prize winners and finalists with distinction (2011, 2013)

Community college	Location	Number of students	Students 25 and older	Underrepresented minorities	Credentials in career/ technical fields
CUNY Kingsborough Community College	Brooklyn, NY (urban)	25,425	22%	48%	26%
Lake Area Technical Institute	Watertown, SD (small town)	1,503	20	3	82
Miami Dade College	Miami, FL (urban)	95,166	37	85	30
Santa Barbara City College	Santa Barbara, CA (urban)	28,763	36	25	24
Valencia College	Orlando, FL (urban)	55,545	30	43	17
Walla Walla Community College	Walla Walla, WA (rural)	8,635	54	19	64
West Kentucky Community and Technical College	Paducah, KY (small town)	10,878	45	7.9	67

Source: U.S. Department of Education Integrated Postsecondary Data System, 2011.

programmatic success—are not perfect, and probably never will be, given the enormous number of variables associated with delivering a community college education. But that cannot prevent us from rigorously evaluating community college success using whatever data are available and finding new ways that entire colleges can address the urgent need to improve community college student outcomes.

The core premises of this book are, first, that even in differing contexts, there are important practices and policies that are associated with high levels of student success in completion, learning, and post-graduation success, including for underrepresented minority and low-income students; and second, that if professors, staff, and leaders at more institutions—no matter their context—examine and learn from those practices, students will benefit greatly.

The book is organized into five chapters. The first four align with the four-part definition of success used by the Aspen Prize: completion, equity, learning, and labor market outcomes. These chapters discuss the importance of community colleges making progress in each of these four areas, provide examples of how colleges have succeeded, and lay out the complexities of measuring that success. The final chapter discusses the critical role leaders play within those community colleges that have achieved exceptional student outcomes.

No single practice or policy featured in this book can be shown with absolute certainty to have improved student outcomes. But the high and significantly improving levels of success these community colleges have achieved for students in completion, equitable outcomes, learning, and labor market success after graduating are simply too different from those at similar institutions to be accidental. Failing to act on them risks delaying progress that could help millions of students who enter community colleges hoping to get an education that will give them opportunities to work and support their families—something too few of them actually receive today.

We owe it to today's and tomorrow's community college students to acknowledge that *some colleges do better than others*. Most importantly, we owe it to every incoming generation of community college students to understand and replicate whatever it is that has allowed exceptional colleges to achieve great outcomes for students.

1

COMPLETION AND TRANSFER

Creating Clarity in a Culture of Choice

OUR CHILDREN'S SCHOOL DAYS ARE clearly prescribed. They start with a morning bell; there's a fixed schedule of classes, lunch, and recess; then the bus takes them home, where they'll face a specific set of homework assignments. As kids grow older, they're given a bit of choice in the classes they take, but all in all, the path to a high school diploma is pretty well fixed.

Later, as adults, they're likely to have an equally structured routine. Bosses make their expectations clear: here's when you arrive, here's your desk or place on the factory floor, here is what we need from you, here's when you'll go home. Show up five days a week and execute your duties well, and you'll get your paycheck.

In between, young adults are on their own, with none of the structure inherent in K–12 education or the world of work. College students are given a course catalog but generally not much guidance as to which of the myriad choices will lead to what jobs—or even which will get them a specific degree on time. Their classes are scheduled for different hours every semester, with lots of time in between to spend as they wish.

When higher education was reserved for well-off young adults who attended one college from beginning to end, this setup worked fine. Students would figure out in their first semester how to navigate a single campus and then attend classes whenever they happened to be held, filling their free time in libraries or cafeterias, or with clubs or sports, none of which required them to stray far from the direct path between dorm room and classroom. Mostly, they were well prepared for college; if not, they figured it out along the way, drawing on a well of confidence built from years of K–12 success and family expectations. Four years in, they'd get a degree.

Translating that haphazard system to the community college sector has failed, for many reasons. Few of today's community college students look anything like their four-year counterparts from prior decades. They almost never live on campus. Many have their own kids. About three-quarters have jobs; over a quarter work full-time.[1] Between classes, students are often rushing off to workplaces or day care centers that might not be able to accommodate a Tuesday/Thursday class schedule one semester and Monday/Wednesday/Friday the next. Of equal significance, three in five students entering community college arrive unprepared to do college-level work in at least one core subject: math, reading, or writing.[2]

And few community college students finish their degrees where they started. If they leave one community college for another or move on to pursue a bachelor's degree—as an estimated 33 percent of community college students do at least once—things get even more difficult.[3] A new course catalog replaces the old, and everything else often changes too: registration processes, course prerequisites, and services from tutoring to guidance to financial aid. Not surprisingly, in addition to the 24 percent of students who graduate within six years from the same public community college where they started, only 12 percent of students who start at community colleges complete a degree anywhere else within that time frame.[4]

That community colleges would face these challenges was, in a sense, inevitable. A central idea behind the creation of community colleges was to expand the number of Americans who go to college, including many more low-income and minority students. That has happened. Since the 1960s and 1970s, when the number of community colleges in the nation grew substantially, the percentage of African American and Latino students attending college has increased dramatically. The participation of African American and Latino students in higher education grew from 13 percent of all postsecondary students in 1976 to 28 percent in 2010, largely accounted for by community college enrollment.[5]

Wider access is good news, of course. Yet these students' economic strains and academic underpreparation have translated into much lower levels of student success. A community college student who is attending college for the first time and carries a full-time course load has at best a one-in-four chance of graduating within three years.[6] Rates for part-time students are even lower.[7]

The community college sector has in the last decade increasingly rallied around the pursuit of higher graduation rates. National philanthropies were among the first to express the goal of substantially increasing the number of Americans with a valuable postsecondary credential; now it is championed by President Obama and reflected in federal and state policy.[8] Because community colleges are relatively affordable, and because their completion rates have been so low, policy makers are leaning on them to move quickly toward meeting these goals.

But how can institutions filled with millions of students who have historically succeeded at the lowest rates lead the charge to higher completion rates? As community colleges attempt to improve graduation rates, the most effective among them acknowledge that their students have little framework for understanding the actual value of completing a college degree as quickly as possible or navigating the often-opaque world of course and program choices. Two goals emerge as critically important: creating clearer pathways to community college credentials and bachelor's degrees, and ensuring that students make better choices along the way.

In general, how programs are structured is important to whether students complete them. Do they know exactly which courses get them closer to their degrees and which don't? Are they taking the right courses to graduate and, for many, transfer to a four-year college? To improve completion rates, community colleges cannot simply help students finish certain courses, such as developmental reading or the often-avoided college-level math.[9] Rather, they must provide clear pathways *all the way* to a degree or certificate. Students who enter into a specific program of study, with a clearly delineated course sequence, have a better chance of completing degrees than those who wander through the curriculum with no roadmap.[10]

That structure is not uncommon in community colleges' career and technical education programs. Several exceptional colleges named Aspen Prize finalists designed technical programs with defined and consistent schedules, leaving little chance that students will become sidetracked. The end result: very high completion rates. Creating such structure is not so simple in general education programs, whose students typically can choose from a wider course catalog, have more discretion in what they select, and are often less clear, from the start of school, about where they want to wind up. Still, effective community colleges work to steer liberal arts majors toward good choices, by advising them early and often about course and program selection, encouraging them to devise plans for completion, establishing rules and incentives and even a unique technological roadmap, and monitoring their progress along the way.

TECHNICAL PROGRAMS: BUILDING STRUCTURES FOR SUCCESS

Lake Area Technical Institute (LATI) in Watertown, South Dakota, is a national role model for how a deeply structured approach to technical programs can serve the goal of degree completion. LATI serves a far-flung rural population of fifteen hundred students. When students arrive there, they enroll in a program of study. Selecting that program from among the thirty the school offers is generally their last significant choice at the school.

Each program has a fixed series of courses, which students attend all day with a cohort of classmates. Seventy-six percent of first-time, full-time students complete their degrees within three years—an exceptional success rate, exceeding those of community colleges that offer the same programs in a looser format. We may never have the kind of rigorous research needed to know what precisely accounts for these outcomes. But a few elements stand out.

The Road Ahead Is Clearly Marked

LATI students tend to enroll with much clearer goals than do general education students at other colleges. More often than not,

15

they report knowing for certain what they want to do when they arrive on campus, from the automotive technology student who had hoped to work on cars since he was seven years old to the aviation maintenance student who enrolled after getting a bachelor's degree so he could do hands-on work that would lead to a job. This clarity can't be invented, of course, but replicating the success of such technical programs may require attempting to increase the number of students who have clear career goals.

Once a student shows up with a goal, the pathway to achieving it is clearly marked. "They all have a graduation plan from day one," says Deb Shepard, LATI's president. "They don't pick their classes." There are only two reasons LATI students fail: they don't show up, or they don't master the required competencies. Students don't have the chance to select the wrong courses or be denied them because of space restrictions. They can see precisely what each class contributes toward their degree or credential. And because their schedule is consistent throughout the two years of their programs, they can plan for out-of-school jobs with certainty.

Instructors Have a Stake in Program Completion, Not Just Course Completion

In the best of worlds, all community college professors care about whether each of their students completes a degree. In reality, though, their responsibility to their students usually ends with the final exam. Few have the ability (or the incentive) to know what happens to their students once they leave their classrooms.

General education faculty are less likely than career tech faculty to keep track of their students once they've left school as well— they don't tend to have students in class more than once or twice, and the students' goals, and thus endpoints, vary widely. In structured technical programs, however, faculty are apt to know their former students' graduation and job placement rates, as well as where individuals end up. This is especially true when cohorts progress through programs in lockstep, as at LATI.

In part, the career tech faculty know this information because it is factored into compliance with accreditation and federal Perkins Act funding, external requirements not applicable to general education programs. For instructors at exceptional community colleges, which achieve strong outcomes for graduates, these aren't just checkboxes to tick off; they are often powerful drivers of continuous improvement. While the way programs are structured makes a difference in achieving higher success rates, so do externally defined standards that help faculty focus on completion and post-graduation success.

Instructors Become Counselors

LATI instructors see their students every day, not just for a couple of hours on Mondays and Wednesdays. They can't help but know their progression as well as their problems. When an LATI student fails to show up for class, she can be sure she'll get a phone call from her instructor. When a student is distraught, his instructor will find time in the seven-hour day to check in and discover what is wrong. Contrast this with community college guidance counselors, whom students must seek out and who are often overburdened with high caseloads. Given their intense proximity to students, LATI instructors' keen attention to outcomes is natural. "You're so close to your students," says LATI agriculture instructor Brian Olson. "We like to see a 100 percent [job] placement rate. When you get 98, you feel bad about the 2 percent."

Tech-oriented community colleges tend to have higher completion rates than comprehensive ones. But the LATI model is harder to replicate in general education degree programs, which often offer hundreds of options from which students can choose in order to fulfill their requirements.

TRADITIONAL PROGRAMS: GETTING STUDENTS ON TRACK EARLY AND KEEPING THEM THERE

General education programs are just that: general. At community colleges, the core requirements for associate's degree programs in liberal arts are structured much like the first two years of four-year colleges. A degree requires the completion of some specific courses, options to take others from among a plethora of choices, and the flexibility to apply those credits to a host of majors. This flexibility means that community colleges have a greater burden to guide general education students so they don't wander through courses without clear-cut goals or pathways (something much less likely for students in career and technical programs).

Given the complexities of embedding structure into liberal arts programs, community colleges aimed at general education degrees and transfer rely on a variety of strategies to get, and keep, students on track.

The Intake Process Is Streamlined

Even before beginning their first course, students arriving on community college campuses often struggle. The process of registration and applying for financial aid often involves waiting in long lines, so they may begin courses without securing financial aid (which may never come) or choose courses they don't need. To alleviate this problem, several colleges have revamped the intake process in thoughtful, efficient ways. One of the most impressive is Mott Community College in Flint, Michigan. For years, starting the semester at Mott was an ordeal for students, who walked themselves through several stops around campus, standing in lines for hours at a time. Not anymore. Now students go to one new, inviting building, which houses the registrar, advising, financial aid, career services, and more. Students stop at an information desk to be directed to precisely the services they need. They are given numbered tickets and always know their wait times, thanks to television screens around the building. While waiting, they socialize or do work at comfortable armchairs and tables. (The waits are shorter, in part because calls are now routed to a call center, freeing office workers to focus on getting students on track rather than on answering constantly ringing phones.) Students can even register themselves at one of several computer terminals, manned by proctors ready to answer questions. "We don't want students to not be successful in the enrollment process, because then they never get to the classroom," says Troy Boquette, dean of student services.

Students Cannot Add a Class After It Starts

At Valencia College in Orlando, Florida, an Aspen Prize winner, data showed that students who enrolled in a class after it had already started were the least likely to complete the semester. Sandy Shugart, Valencia's president, says that those numbers forced officials to ask themselves a question: "What will it take to make the first minute of the first day of the first class a learning minute?" The school adopted a philosophy and set of intertwined policies it calls Start Right.

Students are no longer allowed to add courses after the first day of class. Admissions, enrollment, and advising timelines were moved up to give students enough time to register for the courses they need. For students who miss the enrollment deadline, the school created condensed versions of a dozen or so crucial classes that begin a month into the semester.

Student Success Courses Are Required

Most schools offer student success courses, which teach life skills, such as time management, and study skills students may not have gained during their K–12 years. Only some schools actually have made such courses mandatory for some or all students, after seeing how they improve student outcomes.

At Valencia, data showed that taking such courses increased a student's chances of persisting and graduating. So the school began to require that students with the greatest risk of failure—the 40 percent who place into developmental education in reading, writing, and math—take a credit-bearing student success course, which teaches basic skills such as note taking and time management. In some cases, student success is formally linked with a developmental class, with a pair of teachers who trade off instruction and a cohort of students who attend both courses together. Valencia officials believe that student success courses contributed to the increase over a decade in the college's five-year degree completion rate for developmental students, from 19 percent to 25 percent.

At Miami Dade College, 75 percent of students, including everyone who tests into at least two developmental classes, take Student Life Skills. Course instructors cover traditional study-skills topics, such as where to sit in class to best pay attention and how to seek help from a professor online; more important, perhaps, they help students select a major and create a related education plan.

"It allows students to see an endpoint," says Rene Garcia, Miami Dade's director of enrollment management. "Especially for those who are in remedial work, sometimes they feel they're never going to get out. And it helps to say, 'If you do A, B, and C this semester and next semester, you're free.'"

Students Are Helped to Define Their Path

Miami Dade is not the only school getting students to envision their future from their earliest days at the college. At Valencia, students are encouraged to lay out their goals—for Valencia and beyond—and how they will reach them through software called LifeMap. A student can see the job and salary prospects, as well as what education is needed, for his desired profession; fill out financial planners down to the last penny of gas money; and, of course, plot out coursework. Valencia's marketing budget used to be spent primarily on getting students into the school; now much of it has been shifted to getting students through. Officials believe so strongly in the power of LifeMap that they advertise it on campus in an engaging campaign "as ambitious as anything we would do externally," says Lucy Boudet, vice president of marketing and strategic communications.

Back-mapping from career to coursework is a key strategy as well at Walla Walla Community College, an Aspen Prize–winning school in eastern Washington. The college partnered with Economic Modeling Specialists Intl. to implement its Career Coach software, which points students to occupations with jobs available in the region, along with salary data, employment trends, educational requirements, and even specific course recommendations. Once a major is chosen, counselors work with students to plot courses for every semester, all the way to a degree. But support does not stop there.

Progress Is Monitored Along the Way

At Walla Walla, students can't help but know where they stand. Every one of them, even distance learners, must consult with an adviser before registering each quarter. Faculty who supplement the full-time advising staff receive the regular training and resources they need to be able to ensure that students are always taking courses that advance them.

Each week, the student services and information technology departments meet to discuss how they can use technology to improve student success. Among the fruits of that collaboration: anyone helping a student can access an online portal that collects her academic history, goals, plans, progress toward completion, and transcript and other achievement data. A degree progress estimator overlays transcripts with program requirements to show which milestones students have met on their way to completion. A program automatically flags students who left the college but have most of the credits toward their degrees; they're offered a gift card to come to school and meet with a counselor to get back on track. Officials believe this intense monitoring accounts for Walla Walla's better-than-average year-to-year retention rate: 61 percent, compared to about 50 percent nationally.

In Gainesville, Florida, Santa Fe College takes this work one step further with a personalized progress report called My Academic Plan, which is thought to contribute to the college's very high rates of four-year transfer and bachelor's degree attainment.

My Academic Plan configures class schedules for students to select from, based on their degree goals and preferred class times. If they choose a course off their degree path, a warning alerts them. After two semesters, the system insists that undecided students declare a program of study. Students can readily see if their courses count toward transfer to dozens of four-year colleges.

FUNDAMENTALLY CHANGING THE GENERAL EDUCATION DESIGN

While often effective and deserving of broad replication, the improvements these institutions have made to their general education programs are in some ways workarounds: attempts to promote clearer paths in a fundamentally opaque system, one that leaves students a lot of discretion in choosing majors, courses, and schedules. But does that have to be the case? Can community colleges fundamentally redesign their systems to reduce the number of courses and create much clearer, direct pathways—in essence managing student choice—for all majors, including those in general education?

Rigidly defined programs may run against the notion—at least the notion some have—of a liberal arts education. But while students wander, the clock is ticking on their financial aid.[11] And their two-year degree, much less the four-year degree that many imagine (and which generally holds more value for them), becomes more remote.

A student who arrives on campus well prepared, focused, and motivated may be able to navigate this system fairly well. But it's another matter for underprepared students, who are often the first in their families to experience college. Courses chosen without much consideration as to whether they count toward a degree are likely not just to delay graduation, but dramatically reduce a student's likelihood of ever completing a credential.

Understanding this, a few community colleges have begun to move general education liberal arts programs closer to the structured model used by LATI. In 2008, John Mogulescu, senior dean for academic affairs for the City University of New York system, presented Chancellor Matthew Goldstein with several ideas for improving student success, including a new first-year experience for community college students. Having seen several other initiatives lead only to incremental improvements in student success, Goldstein said he wasn't interested. He was "tired of being confronted by exceedingly low graduation rates that we could not seem to improve," Mogulescu recalls. Goldstein challenged him to instead build something entirely new, something that would dramatically change completion rates.

After examining all the options, the system office recommended a new college for the city that would above all else create greater structure and limit course choice, something akin to what is offered at LATI, but outside career and technical education. In the fall of 2012, the New Community College began operations with only six programs of study, each of which prescribes at least 90 percent of all courses for the degree, leaving students to elect no more than six of the sixty credits needed to graduate.[12] The early results have been quite promising.[13]

But not every college can start from scratch. With help from the Bill & Melinda Gates Foundation, nine colleges in three states are trying to create greater structure as part of an effort called Completion by Design, which provides community colleges assistance to increase structure so that more young, low-income students finish school. One of the pilot sites is the nation's largest community college and an Aspen Prize finalist, Miami Dade College, which enrolls more than one hundred thousand students annually.

At the outset of Completion by Design, Miami Dade officials looked at data showing that certain subpopulations were not succeeding: developmental math students on one campus, students who needed to learn English on another. When they looked then not at who struggled but who succeeded, they noticed something important: no matter their program of study, students who completed 25 percent of required courses in their first year were twice as likely to succeed as those who didn't. That led to what Lenore Rodicio, vice president for student achievement, describes as an "epiphany in unison." What students needed, officials realized, were more structured advising and pathways, whether they started out in developmental courses or college-level ones.

Some people worried that fixing pathways would remove too much student choice—until they spoke to students. From students on academic probation and those in the honors program, they heard the same thing, recalls Rodicio: by the time students find out they've taken the wrong courses, it's too late. Students said, "Just tell me what I need to take to complete my degree." Part of the problem with the old structure was that Miami Dade advisers simply could not keep straight what students should take when each could pursue any number of degree options, each with different possible concentrations and hundreds of possible electives.

To narrow down choice is difficult. All faculty members believe their courses impart important knowledge. Getting a set of math professors to agree on which of the dozens of departmental offerings—including their own—is most important for business majors is a challenge. But it's a critical step, and at Miami Dade, it's now in the past.[14] Default pathways have now been created in the five biggest majors, for full-time and half-time students. Together, these pathways enroll 60 percent of the entire student body.[15]

Beginning in the fall of 2013, most students and advisers were given a much better way to select courses. "For the majority of students, it [just requires] transferring those courses listed on the pathway to a student's schedule," Rodicio explains. If a student wants to take an extra course, he and his adviser need only look at the pathway for future semesters instead of guessing which of the thousand courses in the catalog might help him graduate ready for whatever comes next.

SUCCEEDING THROUGH TRANSFER

For most students entering community college, educational goals do not end with a community college credential. They intend to transfer to a four-year college and get a bachelor's degree.[16] Unfortunately, as little as 20 percent make the leap to a four-year college, let alone actually receive a degree there.[17]

Consider the case of Cara Anderson.[18] "I was always good at school," she recalls. She aimed to be an engineer, but after marrying shortly after high school, having two children, and getting divorced, she found herself at the age of thirty-two working as a full-time hostess at T.G.I. Friday's. Unless she did something different, there was little chance of her providing a better life for her kids, and for herself.

So she began a journey to the career she had dreamed of back in high school. The road to becoming an engineer started at the only nearby school Anderson could comfortably afford, Northern Virginia Community College (NOVA). She went about her studies diligently, juggling her work hours, parenting duties, and part-time coursework to earn straight A's in her associate's degree program. After a few years at NOVA, she prepared herself and her family to move two hours away so she could enter Virginia Polytechnic Institute, a highly selective state university with a strong engineering program.

Advisers at NOVA counseled her instead to go to nearby George Mason University, to be closer to family who could help with child care. But Anderson applied only to Virginia Tech, her dream school. When the thin envelope arrived, it was not quite a rejection. Anderson had been accepted, on the condition that she take the final math course she needed as a prerequisite.

But Anderson was registered for a final math course she had been advised to take. The problem: while it met the requirements to enter the engineering program of George Mason, it was the wrong prerequisite for Virginia Tech. It is unclear whether Cara's advisers had misunderstood her plans or had simply been confused about the different prerequisites for engineering programs at different state colleges. Either way, Anderson had to wait an additional full year to enter Virginia Tech, until NOVA offered the math course at a time she could fit into her work schedule.

Cara's story is not unusual. Students across the country make rational decisions—working hard in class and doing everything they think they need to finish their degrees and transfer—only to find out that they went off track. At best, this wastes time and money for students, as they try to make up for course choices that could easily have been set right. At worst, students become frustrated or broke or both, and never transfer at all.

The Important Role of State Policy

As in Virginia, many states allow each four-year college to set prerequisites for entry into the junior year of specific programs. This results in a confounding maze. A student intending to transfer from Brazosport College in Lake Jackson, Texas, to study accounting needs Math 1324 to transfer to Sam Houston State, Math 1325 (but not 1324) to transfer to Texas Southern, or two sections of calculus for University of Texas at Austin. It is not enough for students to know what they want to study; they need to know exactly where they want to study it after transferring.

Across the country, the standard approach to helping students transfer from two-year to four-year colleges is to create *articulation agreements*. These policies assure students that the credits they've earned at a community college will count toward at least the core general requirements of the four-year degree. They often include a defined set of general education requirements that must be accepted by any public four-year college, without regard to where in the state's public college system those credits were earned.

Articulation agreements prevent students from having to take courses twice, which makes sense. But evidence strongly suggests that these policies alone do not significantly increase the number of transfer students.[19] Unless students see many of their peers actually transferring and getting bachelor's degrees, they won't view it as a route worth navigating.

Some state or system policies go further than articulation agreements. For example, Florida, California, Virginia, Pennsylvania, Massachusetts, and Colorado all guarantee students who complete certain associate's degrees a slot in a public four-year college. These guarantees not only send a clear signal to students that a transfer pathway exists, but also create an expectation that the state's four-year institutions will ensure adequate capacity.

Unfortunately, even these guarantees have been insufficient to significantly increase transfer rates. Some have concluded that's because there are too few incentives for individual four-year colleges to accept the additional students. Community colleges cannot do this work alone. State policy makers must make sure that four-year colleges have the space to make transfer available to more than a few lucky community college students.

Economics are a big reason more states should aggressively develop policies aimed at improving the successful transfer from two- to four-year colleges. As states have entered an era of fiscal austerity, they have in recent years decreased funding for higher education. As a result, tuition has risen, putting additional pressure on students and their families.[20]

President Obama, alarmed at this trend, put colleges on notice during a 2012 address at NOVA: "You can't just keep on raising tuition and expect us to keep on coming up with more and more money . . . So what we're saying to states, colleges, and universities—if you can't stop tuition from going up, then funding you get from taxpayers will go down. Because higher education cannot be a luxury; it is an economic imperative that every family in America should be able to afford. That's part of the American promise in the 21st century."[21]

Ensuring strong transfer pathways can bring down college costs for both states and students. In 2012, Robert Templin, president of NOVA, proposed a plan to increase access to bachelor's degrees for low-income students by reducing the cost of a bachelor's degree paid by the state and by families by over 40 percent. The idea: students complete one year of college while in high school through Advanced Placement (AP) Courses or dual enrollment, spend two years at the community college, and complete their last year at a public four-year college.

Since Templin proposed this solution, two public universities have agreed to consider these "three plus one" arrangements in a few career fields—nursing, information technology, fire science— but others have not been willing to participate at all. At least part of the reason probably has to do with money. Public four-year colleges receive funding based on how many students are enrolled. Essentially ceding the junior year of enrollment to community colleges would mean fewer students, and thus fewer dollars.

As long as four-year colleges are free to decide how many transfers they take, and as long as funding flows to individual institutions based on their enrollments, policies aimed at helping students successfully transfer will have limited effect. Educating an underclassman is less expensive than educating a junior or senior, largely because entry-level courses tend to be bigger and thus cost less per student in professor salaries, classroom space, and so on. And at colleges with selective admissions, admitting transfer students is generally thought to reduce the size of the entering freshman class, which can raise the ire of numerous constituencies.[22]

It is possible that four-year colleges may only significantly increase the number of transfer students accepted if they are forced to. The state that has come closest to creating such a mandate is California, whose state university systems give admissions priority to community college alumni over other transfer students and are obligated to plan enrollment so the student body is composed of 60 percent upperclassmen and only 40 percent freshmen and sophomores.

Alternatively, policy makers can make it more fiscally worthwhile for colleges to work with other institutions to create more efficient and effective transfer pathways to bachelor's degrees—pathways that under current funding systems may not be viewed by four-year colleges as economical, but provide savings for states and families. One way might be through the performance funding systems some states are moving toward, which reward colleges for graduating students rather than just enrolling them; those systems could perhaps provide a premium for four-year colleges to enroll and graduate community college transfers.

What Community Colleges Can Do

No matter what policies a state promulgates, successful transfer programs are built more on practice than policy. Two-year and four-year colleges must work closely together if significant numbers of community college students are to earn bachelor's degrees. Exceptional community colleges demonstrate how a strong institution-level commitment to making transfer work can help thousands of community college students reach their goal of obtaining a bachelor's degree.

Exceptional community colleges with high rates of transfer have achieved that success by creating clear pathways into particular colleges, hosting a four-year college on their campuses, or engineering agreements so that large numbers of slots are reserved for their students in four-year schools. They create rigorous programs designed to prepare students well for upper-division bachelor's degree work. And they create systems to make sure students are on track.

At Aspen Prize–winning Santa Barbara City College, about half of entering full-time students transfer to a four-year college, and over half of those receive a bachelor's degree within six years of entering the community college (including those who attended part-time). At Valencia College, the number of students who have completed degrees and then transferred to four-year schools increased dramatically over the last seven years. How these colleges achieved such remarkable outcomes offers lessons to other colleges and systems.

Offer guarantees to a specific four-year college. When admissions at the University of Central Florida (UCF) were growing more selective, and the school, traditionally a commuter college, was starting to accept more outsiders, leaders from Valencia and other local community colleges worked with UCF to develop a program, called DirectConnect, which guarantees admission to students who received an associate's degree at their schools. (Conversely, community college students cannot transfer to UCF *without* an associate's degree.) UCF has a facility on Valencia's main campus, so students need not leave to get a bachelor's degree. But that's not all: staff from UCF and Valencia collaborate to advise students, align curriculum, and track student success. Valencia's leaders know that it doesn't matter how well students who want a bachelor's degree did at the community college if they aren't succeeding at UCF.

Prepare students with rigorous academics. Four-year colleges are more eager to open their doors to community college graduates when those students are rigorously prepared. Santa Barbara City College builds its courses with an eye to the academic standards of the highly selective four-year schools its students aspire to. Its writing center, for instance, is staffed not by peer tutors but by trained professionals. Students don't leave tutoring sessions there with an edited paper; they leave with new skills to tackle assignments confidently on their own. Throughout the college, "faculty puts a tremendous emphasis on making sure students do a lot of writing and critical thinking," says Provost Jack Friedlander. After transfer, he says, "our students come back and tell us they were really well prepared, that our courses were as challenging or more challenging than those at their transfer institutions—even Berkeley and UCLA."

Of course, that can't be true everywhere. Community college professors and leaders often assert that their courses are just as rigorous as four-year college courses. While there can be little doubt that the opposite view on four-year campuses is fueled as much (or more) by elitism as by a clear-eyed assessment of learning, research shows that not all college courses are equally rigorous.[23] Not every community college prepares students well for their junior year.[24] But more will need to if community colleges are to more routinely overcome the all-too-common bias against their students.

Advise students effectively.   National estimates suggest that, on average, each community college counselor works with at least one thousand students.[25] With that kind of caseload, it's easy to see how students can fail to get the information they need to ensure a smooth transfer. Effective colleges put considerable resources into matching each student with the right transfer options and the courses that will get her there. Advisers at Santa Barbara City College's transfer center, which added staff even as the college made budget cuts elsewhere, take students on college tours, help them plan their course schedules based on the requirements of their target colleges, and even connect them with counselors from those schools who can advise them by email and video chat.

When advising students who aim to transfer, community colleges must make sure they are directing them not just to any four-year college, but to ones that will serve them well. Counselors should discourage students from transferring to schools with low graduation rates, where they have poor chances of success, and instead point them toward the most selective colleges they can get into that offer the programs they want.[26]

From a student's perspective, completion can mean several things depending on where she is headed after community college. But no matter the destination, finishing a credential is better than leaving empty-handed. More community colleges must figure out not just how to improve existing structures, but also how to invent new ones, if they are to increase the chances that many more students complete college.

A NOTE ON MEASUREMENT

Completion

As colleges move to make progress on completion and transfer, they have to do a better job of measuring whether they are succeeding—which first means coming to a common understanding of how to define and measure success in the first place.

In a way, completion rates—more than learning and labor outcomes—are easily measured. Every U.S. college can count the number of students on campus and the number of degrees and certificates it awards each year. While the systems used by different community colleges to measure course and program completion vary considerably in sophistication and usability, baseline information on student enrollment and degrees conferred exists everywhere.

Because such data can be gathered at the institutional level, it can also be aggregated at the state and federal levels. As a result, graduation rates can be used to assess progress against institutional, state, and national goals. This almost certainly explains why graduation rates—rather than any other measure—are today the predominant outcomes focus in higher education.

But actually making sense of graduation rates requires understanding a few fundamental variances among community college programs and groups of students.[27] Most importantly, three sets of factors appear to significantly impact graduation rates:

- *Level of preparation.* Research, and common sense, suggest a significant correlation between the level of preparation when students enter college and the likelihood of graduating.[28] Using such information to understand success rates among students at a particular college is not difficult, as colleges typically have a standard way of assessing remedial needs. However, because community colleges employ different systems for assessing preparation levels of entering students, comparing results across colleges can be quite difficult.

- *Program type and length.* There is strong evidence that completion rates at community colleges are higher for career and technical education programs than for associate's degrees in general education. The average graduation rate for first-time, full-time students in the quartile of community colleges that offer the highest percentage of career tech credentials is 29 percent, while the graduation rate is 21 percent for the quartile with the lowest percentage of career tech credentials.[29] While there are many possible reasons for this disparity, colleges and policy makers should recognize it when comparing graduation rates across schools or programs within them.

- *Student characteristics.* Several student characteristics appear correlated to student success at a school, including the percentage of students from traditionally underperforming minority groups, the percentage of Pell Grant recipients, the poverty level of the college's environs, and the percentage of part-time versus full-time students. Understanding whether variances in graduation rates are related to one or more of them can help colleges and policy makers respond better. For example, in Connecticut, data showed that full-time community college students had better graduation outcomes than part-timers. So officials looking to improve their loan packaging process decided to automatically package all students' financial aid under the assumption they'd be full-time. In the years since, the number of full-time students in the state's twelve community colleges has increased dramatically, and their graduation rate more than doubled—an increase officials attribute in part to that switch.[30]

Measuring graduation rates first requires deciding what credential counts. Everyone believes that attaining an associate's degree counts as completing, but agreement ends there. Is it a successful outcome if a student receives a certificate that requires coursework of just one year? If he completes at least a semester at a community college without a degree and then transfers to a four-year college? Should colleges be acknowledged for simply retaining students, and, if so, what about students who spend a year in one community college and then transfer to another?

There is reason to create incentives for students to stay in college, whether at the same school or elsewhere, in light of the enormous number of community college students who drop out after the first year. But just staying in college does not guarantee completion, and moving from one two-year school to another might harm a student's chance at a credential, if credits don't transfer. So it is risky to craft measurement systems that reward schools for simply keeping students enrolled rather than graduating them, which needs to be the ultimate goal.

• • •

Measuring transfer rates is, unfortunately, no less complicated. Even students who aim to transfer when they enter community college don't often follow the straight path of entering community college, finishing an associate's degree, transferring to a four-year college, and then receiving a bachelor's. Some attend multiple community colleges and multiple four-year institutions, sometimes even starting a bachelor's degree before becoming a "reverse transfer" and enrolling in a two-year college. Others, including a growing number of high school students, take just one or two courses at a community college.

Even those on a linear track from two-year to four-year college cross that boundary at different times. In Florida, where state policy explicitly benefits students aspiring to transfer if they already have earned an associate's degree, relatively few students leave community college early. In California and Texas, the opposite is true—at some community colleges, more students transfer to four-year colleges without an associate's degree than get the degree at all.

The field can't even agree on how to define *transfer*. In its main measurement database, the Voluntary Framework of Accountability, the American Association of Community Colleges lumps all transfers together, whether they move from a community college to a four-year college or to another two-year institution. This definition implies that all transfers should be counted as success stories.

On the other end of the spectrum, advocates for increasing degree completion often don't count transfer to a four-year college without a degree as a successful outcome. While it is true that students who get an associate's degree before transferring complete a bachelor's degree more often than those who don't, data show that transferring to a four-year college—with or without an associate's degree—is correlated with higher degree completion rates.[31]

Treating these two kinds of transfer as equivalent does not make sense, nor does counting a student who transfers to a four-year college without an associate's degree as a dropout.[32] A strong definition of community college student success should include all students who transfer from a community college to a four-year college.

When measuring transfer, the field faces one final pragmatic problem: actually tracking students. As the largest investor in public higher education, states could surely keep track of students who stay in their state systems. But some do a better job than others. And with the U.S. government investing tens of billions of dollars in thousands of colleges every year, much of it in the form of Pell Grants, one might expect it to keep track of how well students do when they move from one state to another, or into a private college. Yet the federal government tracks only completers who attend the same college full-time from start to finish. There is a requirement that community colleges report the number of students who transfer from their institution to another, but the reported numbers are considered unreliable.[33]

Many challenges associated with measuring completion and transfer likely will be resolved in the coming years as states, the federal government, and community college associations improve data collection efforts. But even today, community college leaders have access to data that, while far from perfect, offer information critical to benchmarking and improving degree attainment rates.

2

EQUITY AND DEVELOPMENTAL EDUCATION

Confronting the Tension Between
Access and Success

M ANY AMERICAN COLLEGES STRIVE TO educate a diverse population. Community colleges, though, are defined by that diversity. They serve students of all ages, races, incomes, and levels of academic preparation. They serve high school dropouts seeking a GED and valedictorians aiming for graduate degrees. They serve nineteen-year-old immigrants who are the first in their families to graduate from high school and senior citizens who earned advanced degrees decades earlier.

Virtually every community college program is available to every student. While a few, like nursing, require a certain level of mastery prior to enrollment, students who start college underprepared can enter even those programs if they successfully complete prerequisites. Community colleges send a clear message to students: from a one-year certificate in welding to a two-year preparation for a bachelor's in engineering, nothing is off-limits.

Moreover, community college tuition in 2012 averaged $3,000 per year, a fraction of what four-year colleges charge. The lowest-income students could cover that entire tuition with a Pell Grant from the federal government and still have more than $2,000 remaining to pay for books, transportation, or meals. In an age of escalating tuition and mounting student debt, that's an attractive possibility.

Given the large number of underprepared students and today's constrained government resources, though, maintaining this broad access and diversity can be hard for schools. Succeeding with the students they have is even harder.

Imagine a student entering community college with an eighth-grade math level and her heart set on becoming a nurse—a program that is highly competitive and often requires at least twelfth-grade math for a student to even get in. Is her goal realistic at all? If so, how long will it take for her to make it through? What resources should the community college allocate to help her—and will providing them mean that some other needy student is deprived?

Or consider the challenge of a psychology professor who is teaching an introductory course in which some students read at a tenth-grade level and others can easily handle college-level material. What texts should be assigned? Can assignments be made both challenging and accessible for all students? What standards should be used to grade papers and tests?

In 2012, forty of fifty states cut higher education funding, forcing community college leaders to make choices about resources. Which matters most: retraining displaced workers for jobs, providing remedial classes for underprepared students and English for immigrants, or moving students toward an associate's degree in the liberal arts?

Even with constricted funding and many goals, few community colleges are seeking to narrow their mission. And while it could make sense for schools to focus more intently on doing a few things very well, doing so might limit student access. The demand for degrees is growing, and for many students community colleges are the only physically and financially accessible higher education option out there.

Rather than seeking to narrow their mission, then, exceptional community colleges aim to improve outcomes for all students, in all programs. And all community colleges making a concerted effort are generally aware that the students who succeed at the lowest rates are minority and low-income students.

There are almost as many approaches to helping these students as there are community colleges. Some programs are targeted to specific populations: academic and social support groups for black males, scholarships for low-income single parents, a structured pathway to increase the number of Latino students who enter college-level courses.[1] Other schools have centers to assist anyone in need, such as the Single Stop programs, which connect students at seventeen community colleges nationwide with financial aid, tax refunds, transportation vouchers, food stamps, and other forms of assistance. And the list goes on.

Given the constraints many community college students face—living in poverty, say, or being the first in their family to attend college—schools are wise to lift barriers through these kinds of supports. But removing obstacles to a degree or certificate does not ensure that enough students will actually earn one.

And when colleges examine academic success data for low-income and minority students, a single enormous challenge sticks out: low success rates for students who enter but are not academically prepared. Of the 60 percent of students who enter community college with developmental needs, only a quarter of them earn a degree within eight years.[2] That means that 45 percent of the entire community college population enters behind *and* never gets a degree. It is simple math: overall outcomes cannot improve very much, nor equity gaps be closed, unless students who enter college behind succeed at much higher rates.[3] And community colleges cannot be truly equitable institutions until they have vastly improved the success rates of students entering who need remediation.

PERSISTENT EQUITY GAPS

Low-income and minority students are significantly less likely than others to receive a college degree. By age twenty-six, more than half of all students from families in the top income quartile have gone on to earn a bachelor's degree, compared to only 10 percent of those from families in the bottom income quartile.[4] Similarly, 31 percent of white adults have a bachelor's degree or higher compared to only 18 percent of African Americans and 13 percent of Hispanics.[5]

For the foreseeable future, the white population in the United States is expected to hold steady, while birth rates for minorities will continue to grow. Consequently, the projected 13 percent increase in college enrollment over the next decade will be driven primarily by increases in Hispanic students (a projected 38 percent increase) and African Americans (26 percent).[6]

If current attainment rates hold steady, merely providing these students greater access to college will not resolve inequities in degrees attained. As figure 2.1 illustrates, white students who enter college receive both associate's and bachelor's degrees at substantially higher rates than either African American or Hispanic students.

For minority and low-income students, the biggest challenge is remediation. Being African American, Hispanic, or in the lowest third of the income distribution is more strongly correlated with underpreparation than are other student characteristics, including whether a parent has a college degree. Seventy percent of

FIGURE 2.1
College completion by race/ethnicity

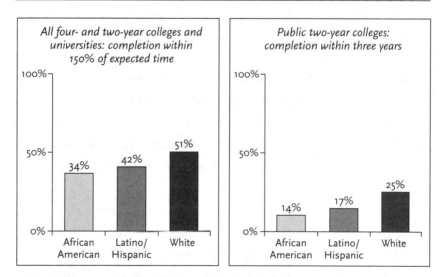

Source: U.S. Department of Education, National Center for Education Statistics, Integrated Postsecondary Education Data System (IPEDS), 2011 Graduation Rate Survey (fall 2008 cohort for two-year colleges and fall 2005 cohort for four-year colleges). Includes all first-time, full-time, degree-seeking students who completed a degree or certificate within three years for an associate's degree or six years for a bachelor's degree.

students in those three groups enter community college needing at least one developmental class.[7]

For the United States to reach the degree completion goals President Obama and others have laid out, success rates will have to improve dramatically among students who enter needing developmental education. Only then can we develop the talent needed to fuel the nation's future economy and give life to community colleges' mission of equity and social mobility.

TACKLING THE REMEDIAL CHALLENGE

In 2011, a study found that students who entered Virginia community colleges with remedial needs were equally likely to succeed in college-level classes whether or not they actually took remedial courses.[8] This result was disturbing, but not surprising. The researchers were comparing students who needed remediation but skipped it with those who took remedial courses delivered in a traditional fashion: with an instructor lecturing two or three days a week and assigning homework. By definition, many remedial students were unsuccessful in their K–12 studies. If these college math and English classes were structured just like their high school ones were, why would we expect students to have done any better?

Most efforts to improve developmental education aim to get students through developmental courses and into credit-bearing classes, often defining a program's success by how many students do so. On one hand, it is hard to argue against that definition of progress. It is certainly good for students to gain the basic skills they should have learned in high school. At the same time, though, that is not why students go to community college. They want the education and skills that will get them a decent job they can keep. There is no evidence that completing remedial sequences—as traditionally structured—gives students a good chance of completing a degree and getting a decent job.

Recognizing this, many community colleges are working hard to offer something different—something that is engaging and relevant, meets students where they are, and doesn't take forever. In other words, they are trying to move students not just through remediation but into and through a degree or certificate program, as quickly as they can.

Several promising strategies have increasingly been adopted by community colleges nationwide: combining computer-delivered modules with tutoring to accelerate success, better assessing remedial needs in the first place so students take only what they really need, and embedding developmental courses into credit-bearing ones. We don't yet know whether these approaches work.[9] But we know community colleges will never get anywhere if they don't take bold chances.

Speeding Things Up: Modular Remedial Delivery

Many community colleges and a few state systems, including Tennessee and Ohio, have abandoned the old way of delivering developmental math education and replaced it with what is known as the *emporium* model, a blend of technology and tutoring that allows students to move at their own pace. Courses are redesigned so that a semester's worth of content is broken down into a series of smaller modules. Those modules are delivered online, in a computer lab available to students five to seven days a week. When students get stuck, they can get help from professors or high performing students trained as tutors.

The computer provides regular opportunities for students to solve problems, administers frequent tests, and gives regular feedback on what students got right and what they still need to learn. It feeds student performance data to faculty, enabling them to monitor progress and provide targeted assistance.

Notwithstanding positive results on some campuses, the jury is still out on the overall effectiveness of the emporium model. For example, in the first year of implementation at West Kentucky Community and Technical College in Paducah, students who completed emporium classes got better scores on the same tests as students who had taken traditional courses, but course retention rates were no better than before. Longer-running programs in Tennessee have shown more positive outcomes in both retention and learning.[10]

Kingsborough Community College in Brooklyn, New York, is trying out a number of ways to accelerate developmental coursework. Students who just missed the cutoff for college-level work can take English 101 classes with the help of tutors. Compressed, intensive courses teach a semester's worth of developmental math in as little as a week. Another initiative, part of a pilot at several community colleges in the City University of New York (CUNY) system, has clearly improved success for the most underprepared students. Called CUNY Start, the program enrolls students who need remediation in fifteen to eighteen weeks of intensive instruction, twenty-five hours a week, to cover material that otherwise takes several semesters to finish. Before they teach in the program, professors are trained for a full semester in delivering an entirely new developmental curriculum based on engaged inquiry (rather than rote memorization). Research has found that students in this program complete developmental education at much higher rates. Specifically, 55 percent of CUNY Start students gained proficiency in reading (compared to 30 percent from the comparison group), 62 percent improved in writing (versus 25 percent), and 54 percent improved in math (versus 12 percent). And nearly a quarter of students who enter needing remediation in all three areas have no remedial needs after completing the program.[11]

Pinpointing What's Needed: Better Diagnostics

Most reforms in remediation deal with how to deliver the material. But a growing number of initiatives are instead focused on how to define and measure the problem. The fundamental question: are current assessments and requirements placing students in remediation they don't need?

Differentiated requirements. In 2007, community college leaders in Virginia decided that the developmental education system was so broken that it was foolish to think they could fix it incrementally. So they completely revamped it. As Glenn DuBois, the chancellor of the Virginia Community College System, recalls, they decided at the time that they couldn't "do any worse."[12]

The first challenge was developing a new remediation system for math, the subject community college students struggle with most. In most community colleges, remedial math needs are determined by a high-stakes test meant to reveal whether students have mastered a single, linear sequence of math knowledge, starting with fractions and ending with Algebra 2.

At some colleges, students are held to the exact same standard on this test whether they aim to earn a higher degree in physics or a certificate in massage therapy.[13] Virginia community colleges decided instead that students should take only the developmental coursework they need for the program they will enter. Math is divided into nine modular units, on which students are tested. Only students intending to transfer to a four-year college and major in math and science fields need be deemed proficient in all nine areas to begin college-level work. Liberal arts majors must show only that they know the first five units, while students entering career and technical programs take tests assessing only the basic skills needed for their areas of study.

Early, limited results have been promising. At Northern Virginia Community College, the first of the system's colleges to pilot the intervention, the number of students enrolled in math remediation dropped by 10.5 percent after the new testing system was put in place, and enrollment in college-level math courses increased by 12.2 percent.[14]

In the coming years, the college and system will assess whether students who traditionally entered developmental courses—but no longer do—actually graduate in much larger numbers. If they do, other states and their community colleges will be forced to consider an uncomfortable possibility: innumerable students have long been placed in remedial programs that they didn't need. "I think a lot of the remedial challenge is actually of our own making," says Robert Templin, NOVA's president. Templin, along with other community college leaders in the state, is betting that redefining the problem so it's smaller will be a big part of the solution.

Imperfect assessments. Most community colleges have long used one of two assessments to test entering students for readiness: the Accuplacer, published by the College Board, or Compass, from ACT.[15] But recent research is causing many colleges to reconsider.

Two 2012 reports demonstrated that those tests are used in a way that sometimes leads to radical misplacement, forcing as many as 30 percent of students into developmental courses they simply don't need.[16]

Part of the problem is that these tests are aligned to semester-based courses, so students are assigned to a full fourteen weeks of instruction whether their shortcomings relate to material taught in the first seven weeks, the second seven weeks, just two weeks, or the entire semester. And the tests lump together students with quite different remedial needs. A student who did well in high school algebra many years before and only needs to brush up on forgotten material may be placed in the same math course as someone who failed high school algebra or never took it at all.

Some colleges encourage students to study for the test and even provide them study guides so that if all they need is a brush-up, they'll do okay. This simple, low-cost step can make the difference between a degree taking two years to complete or taking three—or more.

But even if students are well prepared, that doesn't fully help if the tests themselves result in poor placement. Research suggests that evaluating grades from high school transcripts along with standardized tests can improve remedial placement decisions.[17] Colleges across the country are trying to figure out how to amass the staff resources to do this, especially when so many students register for classes at the last minute and about a quarter have been out of high school for many years.[18] But while community colleges in several states are working to remedy weaknesses in remedial assessments, most community colleges continue to use the old system.[19]

Material that matters: combining remedial and credit courses. Students enroll in community colleges enthusiastic to learn about diesel engines, or political science, or the human body. Then they usually find themselves studying only arithmetic and basic writing, in classes that garner them no credits but still cost them money. To students, the work can feel not just boring—a rehash of what they did in high school—but also irrelevant to what they entered college to do.

Some colleges are trying to remedy this by embedding developmental coursework right into credit-bearing classes that move students toward their degrees. Throughout Washington State, schools are implementing Integrated Basic Education and Skills Training, known as I-BEST. The program, originally developed by the state community college system for adult students and English language learners, pairs content and remedial instructors to coteach college-level classes, so students can develop basic skills at the same time they are progressing toward credentials.

Walla Walla Community College offers seventeen I-BEST courses each semester in twelve programs including nursing assistance, law enforcement, and watershed ecology. In watershed ecology, I-BEST versions are offered for required courses that have heavy reading, writing, or math components anticipated to be challenging for students. When Melissa Holecek and Jan Turner cotaught Methods in Fish Biology, a course that gave students credits in both science and writing, Holecek would use the first hour of the class to teach the content, in a lecture or a lab. As she did, Turner would write notes on the board, offer up the Latin root of a tricky vocabulary term, or raise her hand with a question she suspected students had but were too timid to ask. In the second hour, Turner would give the students writing assignments based on the biology concepts they'd just learned. Both instructors graded the work, Holecek for conceptual understanding and Turner for writing competency.

Holecek loved that the class "completely and totally linked to something that interests students," in a way a traditional remedial writing class would not. There's help so that students aren't bogged down, she says, "but the expectations aren't any lower."

Nor are the results. A 2009 study found that throughout Washington, students in I-BEST courses had better outcomes—in persistence, basic skills tests, and completion—than other remedial students.[20]

Based in part on these promising results, a consortium of major community college researchers and advocates in late 2012 recommended embedding developmental education into credit-bearing classes much more often.[21] But it is too soon to tell whether this will work at scale. Acclimating faculty to a new way of teaching underprepared students may be a bigger challenge than anyone thinks. A common refrain from faculty on virtually every campus across the country—two- and four-year schools alike—is that many students are ill prepared for the material they are being taught. As Columbia University, community college researchers have noted, "Faculty are frustrated when students enroll in courses for which they are not academically prepared; in addition to the resulting challenge for the students, faculty find it difficult to teach a wide range of skill levels in the classroom."[22]

Results from attempts to differentiate instruction at the K–12 level are not conclusive. While research has demonstrated that differentiated instruction can help to address the learning needs of students at different academic levels in the same classroom, the training and mastery required by teachers to effectively differentiate instruction has proven difficult to achieve at scale—particularly in the most underresourced schools.[23] That doesn't mean it can't be done in community colleges, and it is too promising not to try more often. But it is too early to declare this the best answer.

Entry standards in lieu of remediation. Some community colleges have figured out a surefire way to eliminate lousy placement decisions and ineffective remedial delivery: don't offer much remediation at all. At Lake Area Technical Institute, leaders have carefully considered what actually is necessary for success and set entrance requirements accordingly for each of the school's thirty programs—ranging from sixth-grade math for cosmetology to college-level math for nursing. Students are steered to programs that suit their level of preparation. If they are accepted into a program but have borderline skills in reading or math, they receive only minimal remediation, tutoring that's completed in a semester over lunch.

In some ways, LATI's program-specific entrance requirements make sense. Given how much time it takes students at other schools to complete remediation before they can work toward a degree, eliminating developmental education removes a central obstacle to student success. Moreover, even if their math and reading levels limit their program choices, most applicants still have access to *some* program. More than 90 percent of students who apply to LATI are accepted into at least one program. Given the school's exceptionally high graduation rate and strong job placement history, LATI is providing real value to the vast majority of students who seek to enter the school. The college is not spending much energy remediating the failings of the K–12 system, but rather focusing all of its resources on delivering high-quality programs.

But LATI's policy might not fly elsewhere. In most community colleges, in all but a few high-demand programs, students are free to pursue whatever degree they want after passing the remediation test. Many community college leaders and faculty fiercely resist the idea that anyone—especially minority and low-income students—should be prevented from pursuing their academic dreams. Insofar as developmental education gives students the leg up they need, it has come to stand for that opportunity.

Reducing the need for remediation. At all educational levels, when students enter underprepared, it's commonly viewed as someone else's fault—and problem. As Sheila Quirk-Bailey, a vice president at Harper College outside Chicago, explains, "Typically, community colleges blame high schools, which blame middle schools, which blame elementary schools, which blame parents. That's the way it goes."

Except when it doesn't. Some colleges have figured out that it is in fact their problem when students arrive underprepared, so laying blame does not help. Rather than waiting for the next wave of students to arrive and be placed in developmental courses, these schools act to prevent that from happening.

A recognized leader in this area is Texas's El Paso Community College. For over a decade, the college has tested nontraditional students, including those who have been out of high school for many years, well before they arrive at college and has provided them refresher courses in math, reading, and writing so they are less likely to fail placement exams. Similarly, a partnership between the community college, twelve K–12 school districts, and the nearby public four-year college provides intensive preparation over the summer to high school students whose test results reveal that they are behind.

The efforts have worked. Between 2003 and 2009, the number of El Paso Community College students needing developmental courses in all three subject areas fell by 15 percent.

Learning from El Paso, Harper College has proven how quickly success can be achieved when community colleges work closely with their local school districts. In 2010, the college developed a partnership with three local K–12 districts, allowing them to share student data and pursue initiatives designed to get students academically ready for college.

The first issue to tackle: over half of entering Harper students, most of them graduates of local high schools, needed developmental math. The partners found that students were far more likely to be ready for college math if they took math in their senior year of high school. So they tested students and advised those who were not on track for college-level work to take senior-year math. While that helped, some students who took the recommended course still were failing the remedial math placement test.

Digging more deeply, the partners discovered a significant misalignment between the content taught in the local high schools and in Harper College for Algebra 2, the final course in the college-ready sequence. Encouraged by senior leaders, high school and college teachers got together to close gaps in course content and create a common final exam, so that a passing grade in Algebra 2 in the senior year of high school guarantees that students enter Harper College ready for college math. Between 2010 and 2012, math remediation rates at Harper dropped by 11 percent.

That some students in the Harper and El Paso programs would eventually enroll in other colleges did not dissuade these community colleges from trying to reduce all students' chances of being placed in remedial programs. Their willingness to dedicate institutional resources to students these colleges might never educate on their campuses stems from a deep and long-standing commitment, starting with the colleges' presidents, to do whatever local students need, regardless of where they are in the education pipeline.

Unfortunately, funding systems provide little incentive for these kinds of partnerships. With few exceptions, state funds for community colleges are meant to be used for students once they are enrolled in community college, not before they arrive. In fact, there is actually a disincentive, because community colleges receive money when they provide underprepared students remedial coursework. Especially in rural areas, where the pool from which to recruit students is geographically limited, enrolling a much smaller number of students can create serious financial challenges.

Policy makers would be wise to reconsider this, and make the kind of collaboration that happened at El Paso and Harper not just economically feasible but desirable. It is a waste of effort, and money, for high schools and community colleges to simultaneously pursue the identical goal of getting students ready for college-level work. Too many students study the same material in high school and then again in college. In an ideal world, educational systems would partner to ensure that remedial needs are prevented, with the assistance of states. Perhaps if community colleges and K–12 systems worked together to minimize the need for remediation and their duplicated efforts were reduced or eliminated, states could redirect some of the savings they would accrue to those institutions, which could use the money to improve student success in other ways.

ENDING REMEDIATION?

In 2012, the national nonprofit Complete College America released a report concluding that developmental education in community colleges needed to be not just radically altered but stopped altogether. "Remediation doesn't work," Stan Jones, the organization's president, said at the time. "We need to stop doing it."[24]

Even the nation's most successful community colleges struggle to graduate students who enter significantly underprepared. For example, over the past decade Valencia College has dramatically increased the number of entering students who finish their degrees; more than half of students now graduate and/or transfer to a four-year college. But for students who started Valencia more than two years behind, the completion rate has barely budged. Not even one in five of those students completes, no matter how long they remain at the college.

Soon after Complete College America released its gloomy report, the Connecticut legislature took up a bill proposing to end freestanding remediation, and ultimately limited students in the state's twelve community colleges to only a single semester of developmental classes. Such moves are threatening to some equity advocates, given that the law is sure to cut off access to many degrees for deeply underprepared students. As researchers for Columbia University's Community College Research Center put it, "It is far from clear . . . that one semester of instruction is adequate to prepare students with very weak skills for a college level course, even with additional supports."[25]

Complete College America has an answer: deeply underprepared students should still enroll in credential programs, but only those requiring lower levels of readiness. But is it fair to restrict students with the lowest rates of community college completion to such career and technical programs?[26] These policies can be seen as a form of tracking, disproportionately shunting low-income and minority students into what are sometimes poor-quality programs. Reacting to similar prescriptions for developing career and technical education tracks in the K–12 context, long-time equity advocate Kati Haycock of Education Trust summed it up succinctly: "I continue to marvel that so many educators can be so clear about what they want for their own children— college, always college—but so comfortable with something else for other people's children."[27]

Ending freestanding remediation has another risk: it could be used as a way to advance efforts to cut taxes and government support for higher education, inevitably having a disproportionately negative impact on access for disadvantaged students.[28] Concerns about such prospects seem reasonable, considering the language increasingly being used to characterize community colleges and remediation as highly inefficient. In 2011, for example, the Texas Association of Business put up a billboard asking whether a local community college was a good use of taxpayer money, given its extremely low graduation rate.[29] More broadly, national reports of late have labeled community college remedial education as a "waste" of billions of dollars.[30]

Indeed, advocates for open access and community colleges have come to expect the worst. For far too long, community colleges have been funded at much lower levels than other higher education institutions, and the recent criticism of developmental education results seems to some like a setup for further funding cuts. Recently enacted legislation in Connecticut that restricts the amount of remedial education community colleges can provide reinforces these concerns.[31] How can community colleges succeed with the least-prepared students if they are not only starved for resources, but if the central tool for catching students up—remedial education—is legislated out of existence?

Still, community colleges have had years to figure out how to improve the success of students entering with developmental needs, and have failed. Continuing to assign students to the same old remedial sequences that take many years to complete (if they are completed at all) makes no sense. "Simply putting [students] in three levels of remedial math is really taking their money and time with no hope of success," Stan Jones has said.[32] "In a new model students *may* fail," he asserts. "But if we continue doing what we are doing—they *will* fail."[33]

How this debate is resolved, in state policy and community college practice, will play a key role in determining whether community colleges can achieve more equitable outcomes. In trying to come up with successful approaches, leaders must consistently examine data to ensure that reforms close the achievement gap for minority and low-income students. The bottom line is that we need more community college students to graduate with high-quality credentials. We cannot achieve that goal unless many more underrepresented students succeed—that is, unless many more underprepared community college students succeed.

At the same time, community colleges will not improve equitable outcomes by continuing to act as though a student who completed the remedial sequences has reached the finish line. Nor will they close achievement gaps if they operate under the idealistic notion that every degree pathway ought to be open to every student. The data don't lie. When seriously underprepared students have only a tiny chance of getting a degree, something must change.

To increase their chances of success, community colleges will almost certainly have to narrow the options for some students. The sooner community colleges come to that realization, the sooner they can engage in the difficult conversations about how much choice should be narrowed and for whom. Only then can much clearer pathways be invented that hold promise to dramatically increase the chances that minority and low-income students who enter college behind ultimately earn a high-quality credential, and land a good job thereafter.

A NOTE ON MEASUREMENT

Equity

No matter what outcomes it is trying to equalize—in learning, in completion, in employment—an exceptional community college consistently collects, analyzes, and thinks through how it will act in the face of relevant data. Leaders and educators at strong institutions set aside time to look at the data and discuss how to improve outcomes for *all* students, but also disaggregate data by race, ethnicity, income levels, and other factors to see whether certain groups are far behind. Even if, for example, degree completion rates are increasing overall, disaggregated data may show they are not rising for certain subgroups of students.

It is important that any reports a college produces reflect both the relative rate and absolute number of students who succeed by subgroup. Commonly, equity efforts focus on closing gaps between the rates at which different student groups complete college degrees and certificates.[34] That's an important goal, but it's not sufficient. Many community colleges have low graduation rates for even their highest performing groups (usually white, Asian, and higher-income students). Aiming to close the gap between, say, an 8 percent graduation rate for one group and a 15 percent rate for another will not help that many students.

In fact, focusing on eliminating gaps without raising overall rates may cause colleges to prioritize the wrong things. For example, data often show that students who register for classes after the first class meets succeed at lower rates than those who register on time. If focused on closing gaps alone, a college might help specific groups by explaining to them why registering on time matters, helping them choose courses early, or providing preferences in the registration process. If colleges eliminate late registration altogether, though, as Valencia College did, they can improve success for all students.

In addition, looking only at rates of student success—and not the number who succeed—could result in a perverse, unintended consequence: reducing access. Specifically, schools could raise minority graduation rates and narrow or even eliminate gaps by reducing the number of minorities—especially the least prepared of them—who enter the college. Say a school has a graduation rate for its one thousand minority students of 20 percent. If the school engineers a student body that leaves out the least prepared five hundred minority students, and one hundred fifty of the remaining five hundred graduate, it has increased its graduation rate to 30 percent, but decreased the number of minority graduates by 33 percent. It is easy to see how improving rates and not numbers can fail to ensure more equitable outcomes.[35]

Alternatively, colleges can appear to raise completion rates by changing who gets counted. For example, for the purpose of calculating graduation rates, some colleges wait until students complete twelve credits before even counting them as possible completers. Such a definition inflates graduation rates by reducing the size of the denominator rather than actually increasing the number of students who complete. To avoid incentivizing such strategies, focus needs to be placed on the actual number of students who complete degrees, not just the ratios of them.

And colleges can't just look within their own walls to determine if they are achieving equitable outcomes for students. They should regularly compare the share of underrepresented students at their school—by race, income, or other characteristics—with the share in their service area. Once they see that they are missing significant populations, colleges can take steps to reach out and ensure that these students enroll.

3

LEARNING OUTCOMES

Engaging Faculty in Change They Understand

I N HER FIRST YEAR TEACHING AT Valencia College, Irina Struganova found that the students in her general physics-with-calculus class were having trouble solving specific calculations related to electrical fields. On one test, every student left the problem blank. When Struganova asked in class where their struggles lay, they didn't have an answer. Students, she says, "do not know what they do not know."

Struganova didn't really either. "I did not know that it was possible my students lacked very simple [math] skills that I could fix," she says, "because I expected they would know this."

At many colleges, whether or not a professor would diagnose this problem—much less fix it—would be left to chance. At Valencia, though, new professors are obligated to work toward improving their instruction, and therefore student learning, in structured ways. As part of what are called *individual learning plans*, tenure candidates at Valencia must conduct at least one "action research project," where they devise a plan to change an aspect of instruction, refine the plan with the help of a facilitator, implement it (ideally against a control group of another course section), and measure how the change impacted student learning outcomes.

For Struganova's project, in 2009, she decided to tackle this mysterious deficiency in her students. For one section of her class, she developed a diagnostic math skills test to administer the first week of class and an assessment to use during the relevant unit to determine which topics students were having the most trouble understanding. She prepared guided solution sheets on the troublesome issue and worked through examples in class. She gave a homework assignment in which students had to mark every step as clear or unclear.

It was time-consuming and stressful to think through the problem, change instruction, and document the results, Struganova says. But she learned a lot about how to diagnose students' skill deficiencies, a lesson she's carried to other concepts, such as torque and electrical circuits. Focusing clearly on student outcomes—through that project, through the in-depth training Valencia provides its professors, and through collaboration with colleagues—has made her a better teacher, she says.

That such attention to instruction is not routine in higher education would strike anyone working to strengthen K–12 education as strange. It's now conventional wisdom in the K–12 world that the most important thing schools can do to improve student outcomes is improve teaching. Some people might talk about how teachers need better training, or smaller classes. Others might say that we must recruit a higher-quality work force in the first place, or that we need better ways to measure teacher effectiveness. Even though they may disagree on the approach, their common priority is unmistakable: the people at the front of class-rooms must be the focus of any efforts to improve.

Yet conversations about improving college education sound completely different. Current national- and state-level strategies to reform higher education center on everything *but* teaching.[1] And these initiatives—from improvements in financial aid to increasing student service delivery to creating better-defined degree pathways to rewarding institutional success through funding mechanisms—*are* important elements of national and state strategies for increasing student success rates in higher education, including community colleges.[2] Collectively, they create external pressure for structural and data-driven reform, and offer specific models and technical assistance networks that colleges can use to achieve higher degree completion rates.

But these reform strategies often ignore the fact that the quality of education delivered on college campuses still depends on faculty, who instruct students either in traditional classrooms or through technology-enhanced formats. It is as though we believe that something magical happens to the educational endeavor when students turn eighteen. Before then, education leaders and policy makers say that we must focus on the quality of the teachers, the supports they are provided, the conditions under which they work, and the ways they are held accountable for student performance. Once students become adults and enter the world of higher education, though, we act as if faculty either don't matter or can't be changed.

Excellent community colleges reveal that the opposite is true. The nation's best institutions work hard to improve teaching and learning, by engaging educators in the process of measuring how much students learn and devising ways to improve teaching accordingly. In the end, achieving strong student outcomes overall requires deliberate efforts by faculty to improve student learning.

One reason for this conclusion may seem obvious: teaching faculty are the people with the most exposure to the students whose learning outcomes we want and need to improve. For the most part, they are the ones deciding what goes into the curriculum, crafting how best to teach content, and ultimately judging how well students perform.

There is an additional reason that a focus on teaching and learning is central to community college excellence, perhaps even more than in a K–12 school. In higher education generally—and community colleges are no exception—faculty exercise significant authority outside the classroom. Community college decision making is highly decentralized, with professors playing an important role in determining everything from who gets hired to what programs are developed and maintained to the rules regarding what they and their colleagues can and cannot do.

For this reason, educators must be fully engaged in the process of improving student outcomes, not just for teaching to improve, but for governance to be fully aligned with student success goals. And efforts to improve teaching and learning are more likely to engage professors than any other area of institutional change.

At exceptional community colleges, professors buy in to the idea that completion is an important end goal, but they also improve teaching, day by day, as a central means for achieving it. This chapter explores how faculty members are engaged in improving student learning at Valencia College and West Kentucky Community and Technical College. With significantly increasing completion rates, these two schools prove that the goal of better learning outcomes can be positively and powerfully connected to the more publicized goal of increasing degree completion. As Sandy Shugart of Valencia says, "If students learn well, deeply, and intentionally, more will complete."[3]

VALENCIA: BECOMING BETTER PROFESSORS FROM DAY ONE

For some time at Valencia, as at many community colleges, faculty were growing increasingly discontented with the system for receiving tenure. Theater professor Michael Shugg recalls how disconnected the process felt from anything that mattered to him and his colleagues. Faculty were required to turn in individual portfolios for review, but the contents, which were the same for everyone, ultimately seemed like a waste of time.

Among the least inspiring elements of the portfolio was providing proof that faculty had completed a series of required orientation meetings with administrators. "If an orientation meeting conflicted with a scheduled class, we were expected to cancel the class," Shugg says. The symbol of how broken the system was: thirty-five new tenure-track professors, Shugg included, were put on a mandated bus tour of the college's campuses, even though "almost all of us had been working at the college as adjuncts for years."

Meanwhile, it was growing increasingly clear not just to Valencia leaders but to faculty that student learning outcomes were inadequate. A report from the college's institutional research office, for instance, showed that students who failed to complete or pass a class actually did worse the second time they took it.

Until this report, "the prevailing attitude was that if the students failed classes, they should just take them again. They would learn the material by being exposed to it a second time," recalls former English professor Helen Clarke, who later become a leader of Valencia's learning initiatives. The data, though, pointed to an entirely different and very disruptive set of facts, forcing faculty to confront an inescapable conclusion: that they themselves might be contributing to student failure and could not expect different results unless they were willing to improve what they did.

So Valencia embarked on creating a new professional development and tenure system designed not just to serve the personnel process but, more importantly, to help every new professor become a better teacher. In 2004, the school introduced the new system, which had at its core the explicit goal of improving student learning. As part of their tenure portfolios, professors develop detailed plans to change their own classroom practice to improve student learning. The process is elaborate: tenure candidates must attend training seminars to learn how to develop their individual learning plans, meet often with tenure review teams and facilitators, and conduct at least one action research project.

Because the new tenure process was required only for newer professors, the suspicion that typically accompanies major reforms, particular from long-timers, was mitigated. Today, more than two-thirds of Valencia's full-time faculty have engaged in the new process, and nearly everyone has served on a review panel for colleagues. "They don't even remember when people were suspicious of it," Clarke says.

This wasn't a mandate from above; rather, it was "a process completely created and implemented by faculty," says Wendi Dew, Valencia's director of faculty development. At excellent community colleges, faculty, staff, deans, and department chairs work together to invent and scale effective solutions to student success challenges. But while leaders don't need to conceive these ideas, they do need to set urgency for improvement, understand which ideas really matter to student outcomes, and provide the conditions for them to succeed.

The new Valencia tenure system was created by faculty, but its long-term success required vital support from the top. Sandy Shugart, four years after becoming Valencia's president, asked Clarke to lead the tenure redesign process with a focus on quality teaching. As faculty invented the system, Shugart provided steady support and resources for the creation of a Teaching and Learning Academy that guides and professionally develops faculty members throughout the tenure process and beyond.

Through the efforts of professors and the support of administrators, "learning-centered teaching" took hold at Valencia, becoming not a catchphrase but a natural way of life. Today at Valencia, that means that it is not enough for professors to know their subject; they have to refine the way they teach so students learn more. Instructors who don't see that as a priority tend to leave the college before they are up for tenure, which means that those who remain are committed to improvement.

And knowledge sharing is written into the tenure process; action research projects must contain a plan for how professors will share what they've learned with their colleagues. The results: action research projects that start small in scale and are then proven successful—a cooperative problem-solving task replacing a lecture, a new form of study group—spread. One math professor replaced a $150 textbook with a $15 one he created, and his students performed just as well with it. Now his book is used college-wide and the faculty senate has made the development of similar, home-grown textbooks a priority. A developmental reading teacher who replaced one-size-fits-all lab assignments with personalized ones saw so much growth in her students that her approach, too, was replicated across her campus.

While Valencia is better known for other initiatives—such as its LifeMap program for helping students develop and stick with a plan for graduating—Shugart is quite clear about what he thinks matters most to Valencia's success: faculty development supported by the Teaching and Learning Academy. "Nothing else this institution does makes a difference if this doesn't happen," Shugart asserted at a 2012 all-campus assembly.

WEST KENTUCKY: A COLLEGE-WIDE CULTURE SHIFT

Evidence emerging from the four-year college sector strongly suggests that collegiate learning outcomes are lagging. In a widely publicized book, *Academically Adrift: Limited Learning on College Campuses* (University of Chicago Press), authors Richard Arum and Josipa Roksa laid out troubling research findings: after completing two years of college, 45 percent of students demonstrated no growth on a test that measured critical thinking, perhaps the most crucial skill we expect higher education to impart. One variable that seemed to matter tremendously to student learning: academic rigor. Specifically, the authors found that students who took courses that required more than forty pages of reading a week and twenty pages of writing a semester improved their critical thinking and complex reasoning skills.[4]

At the same time, the amount of time college students spend studying appears to be decreasing. In 2011, students at four-year colleges spent about fifteen hours a week studying, compared to twenty-four hours for students in 1961.[5] While no comparable national studies have been done in the community college sector, there is evidence that course rigor in community colleges is lacking as well.[6]

To be sure, the assumption held by many administrators and faculty at four-year colleges—especially the most selective ones—that academic rigor is uniformly lower in two-year schools is far too sweeping to be true and runs counter to my personal experience working with high-achieving community college students seeking to transfer to selective four-year institutions.[7] However, it's not unusual for faculty to note the disparity in levels of preparation between students they had previously taught in the four-year sector and those they taught on two-year campuses.[8] Their experience is borne out by fact: it is estimated that nationally, 60 percent of students entering community college need remediation, more than twice the rate for those entering four-year colleges.[9]

College presidents, deans, and individual professors all deal with a complicated challenge: how to maintain access for students—some of whom are underprepared—while still maintaining a level of rigor that ensures that graduates leave college well equipped for what comes next. In the absence of creative solutions, it can be tempting to simplify coursework. "A lot of colleges and high schools definitely feel the pressure to spoon-feed students—hand out study guides that tell them exactly what they need to know, dumb down the curriculum," says Kim Russell, the English program coordinator at West Kentucky.

Excellent community colleges are driven by a different kind of pressure, an internal culture that drives professors to aim for high levels of student learning. Any school that aims for greater rigor and improved student learning all around needs to take a coherent, institution-wide approach. As Russell puts it, "Instead of griping about the [underprepared] students we had, we have had to make them into the students we want them to be."

Leveraging the Power of Data

Engaging faculty in an authentic process of continuous improvement centered on classroom practice is a difficult task. Faculty have long been exceptionally autonomous in their work, drawing on the honored tradition of academic freedom. Professors want their expertise respected; they want to be able to teach and grade how they see fit; they don't want to be subject to direct comparisons with their colleagues.

For individuals to give up a measure of autonomy, they must first be convinced there is a compelling reason to do so. In the case of community colleges, that reason often begins with a deep sense of despair about the status quo.

Countless students would arrive at Maria Flynn's developmental reading class at West Kentucky and tell her they were going to be nurses. But it occurred to Flynn that at the nursing program's graduation a few years later, she didn't see any of them walk the stage. So Flynn looked at the data. She found that only one student who began in the lower of two levels of remediation ever made it into the nursing program. "I was crushed," Flynn says. "They're so hopeful: 'I'm going to be a nurse. I'm going to make a difference.' And they weren't getting there."

Later, after Flynn had become dean of developmental education, and she and a colleague came back from a conference with a new way to calculate program attrition, she was faced again with disturbing data: of the roughly forty students who began the first of two levels of developmental writing in fall 2009, only six had passed college-level English three semesters later. Up to that point, Flynn says, reform proposals in her department had been met with lots of pushback from faculty, full-time and part-time. But having the numbers in front of them—embarrassing numbers—created a new sense of urgency. "The picture was so stark that there was nothing you could say about it," Flynn says.

The first step toward student learning reform, and getting faculty engaged in the process, is identifying that there is a serious problem. Maria Flynn knew something needed to be done when she looked on the graduation stage, but she could get others on board only when she translated her observations into clear numbers.

Collaborating to Set Learning Goals

As part of a new continuous improvement effort at West Kentucky, Maria Flynn had to evaluate her developmental reading program's track record and make plans to improve it.[10] In assessing the developmental education outcomes, she had to confront a difficult fact: she and her colleagues were not delivering a consistent product. Students were getting passed on to English 101 with skills so low they were a perpetual source of complaint from instructors teaching college-level classes (and a source of defensiveness for the developmental teachers). Different instructors held students to different standards.

This was evident when Flynn gave all the developmental writing instructors seven essays to grade; they marked the same essays with wildly different grades. Two weeks later, they were asked to assess the same essays again. Not only were the grades still all over the place, but only one person gave the same grade she had given before.

So Flynn and her colleagues had to address the question every college must answer if it is to improve learning outcomes: what should students learn? In technical programs, defining and measuring this is usually an easier task. Dental hygienists must know how to create impressions, nursing students must insert catheters, diesel mechanic students must diagnose fuel system problems—all activities professors can watch and easily assess.

But in the liberal arts, establishing the learning outcomes that students will need in order to be ready for the next stage of education—or life and work after college—is more complicated. Students completing general education associate's degrees are headed in many different directions. And a dozen professors of the same subject may have a dozen disparate ideas of what students should take away from their courses.

Flynn addressed this by asking the English 101 instructors what they thought a successful essay should look like. "We came to realize that we didn't have consistent expectations," says Kim Russell, who had recently taken charge of the English department. Punctuation, sentence structure, consistent point of view: "What really, really mattered to one of us, the others thought, 'I can work with that.'"

Flynn then asked each English 101 instructor to rank a list of skills in order of importance. From the results, and information about which skills were weighted more heavily on the ACT, she and her colleagues built a grading rubric to be used with all writing assignments. Students, Russell says, love the rubric because they know exactly what they need to do to improve. Faculty appreciate having a concrete document to refer to when a student challenges a grade.

What's more, this process—driven by faculty and by a new set of departmental leaders—marked the beginning of a complete culture shift; formerly, faculty in developmental and college-level English at West Kentucky could go months, or even years, without speaking to one another. "We came to the realization that our students were victims of our dysfunction," Russell says. "Now we have this common goal of student success: what can we do, and how can we work together?"

One thing is certain: while college leaders can create a sense of urgency for campus-wide reforms, professors themselves must be an essential part of the work to establish common goals for learning. West Kentucky professors, who initially greeted the work with skepticism, met with consultants on campus and attended training conferences on how to design learning outcomes and rubrics. Because faculty were the ones designing the learning outcomes and rubrics, Flynn says, "if somebody said, 'I don't want to do this,' it was really another faculty member they were insulting—and that didn't go well. It wasn't coming from the top down; it was coming across."

Building in Flexibility

At times, institutional reforms in teaching and learning can abrade professors' sense of academic freedom. Administrators sometimes encounter professors who don't just believe they should be free to teach their material based on certain perspectives or beliefs; they feel they should be able to teach whatever they want, however they want. So, at the outset, it's important to build both flexibility and autonomy into the process of devising learning outcome measures, as West Kentucky did.

The West Kentucky outcomes must be tied to the state community college system's general education competencies: communicate effectively, think critically, learn independently, and examine relationships in diverse and complex environments. But the professors in each department, working together, define the specific outcomes for each common course, come up with clear and concrete grading rubrics, and create questions they'll all give on their assessments.

Computer science instructors have selected ninety-one common questions and tasks for the final exam in their introductory classes, college algebra sections have twelve common questions, introductory psychology courses have a common essay question, and English 101 has a bank of essay questions from which teachers select. Instructors design the rest of their exams individually. While they have to grade the common items according to the rubric and report the results, they each decide how much the common items will count in their students' final grades. "Within the framework of the common assessment, you can work to still put your own stamp on it," says Britton Shurley, an English professor.

In many departments at West Kentucky, faculty look at the resulting data as a team to try to diagnose problems. The first time all sections of introductory computer science gave a common final, three veteran instructors sat down with the results to figure out, question by question, what they taught well and what they didn't. DeeAnn McMullen looked at the spreadsheet and asked Carla Draffen why her results were so much better in the multiple-choice questions about computer concepts. "I know you assigned them to read the chapter," McMullen says. "What activities did you have them do?" Draffen explained her approach: fill-in-the-blank topical summaries, hands-on performance tasks, and quizzes at the end of each textbook section, which she allowed students to repeat three times until they passed.

There are limits to what the computer science professors learned from these data. They didn't know if students were more successful on certain questions because the material was taught well or because the questions were too easy. They couldn't explain a discrepancy between certain test results and performance on classroom tasks. They didn't know if students with A's throughout the semester coasted through the final, coloring the results. Yet data analysis allows for a tangible, compelling starting point for conversations and collaboration about why and what to do next.

Putting Goals on Paper

When a learning-centered system is set up well, professors come to find that it is not just busy work, but an engine of real improvement for their own pedagogy. When Rebecca Brown finished her first semester teaching chemistry at West Kentucky, she sat down to fill out the required report on learning outcomes. What percentage of her students had succeeded in thinking critically? Learning independently? Communicating effectively? Her class was heavy on lab reports and handouts; completing them required just "robot motions," as Brown puts it. Had her students succeeded in the learning outcomes? She couldn't even tell.

So the next semester, Brown added a six-week research project. Students would have to write a proposal to show they could communicate effectively. Conducting the project itself would be an exercise in learning independently. Summative written and oral reports required thinking critically and communicating effectively.

"It made a big difference in my class and for my students," Brown says, one she wouldn't have had the impetus to make without the pressure to measure learning outcomes in black and white. "It was kind of a bold move for me." Her students said they really got a lot out of the projects—and so did she. Now, filling out the learning outcomes chart at the end of the term and seeing how well her students have done serves a different purpose for Brown: "It makes me think, how am I going to improve my teaching for next year?"

Learning from Others

Schools that are serious about improving learning outcomes have come to realize the deep importance of professors getting out of the classroom to take advantage of the wisdom beyond. West Kentucky professors are encouraged to visit other schools, attend conferences, and bring back what they've learned. But it is coaching from colleagues that seems to make the biggest difference.[11]

When Allison McGullion left a corporate job to teach business management and marketing at West Kentucky, she asked for help and was assigned a dental hygiene professor as a mentor, through a structured program at the college. When the pair watched videotapes of her classes together, it was a "reckoning moment," McGullion says. The mentor taught McGullion how to reorganize the desks so her room wasn't so chaotic. She helped her get out from behind the lectern and interact with students. She got her to stop a distracting habit of constantly playing with her pen while she lectured. The two professors couldn't have been in more disparate fields. But, McGullion says, "she had wonderful ideas that I never would have thought of on my own. I became more confident in the classroom."

SCALING REFORM: LEADERSHIP FROM THE BOTTOM AND THE TOP

Even when student success data or other triggers impel administrators to act, faculty can resist reform. Instructors might look at evidence of student outcomes—if they look at all—and protest that other colleges aren't dealing with the same set of students, so comparisons are not valid. Or they might view the data as just one chart among many that get dropped on their desks. So how do successful community colleges get faculty not just to pay attention, but to act?

Overcoming these objections in ways that allow change to scale across entire colleges requires steady and determined leaders who think strategically about remaking culture. Over the last decade, West Kentucky has implemented two major student learning improvement efforts: the development and meaningful assessment of student learning outcomes, and an initiative to improve reading skills. The president and her senior team took a careful approach to presenting these changes. To implement the first wave of reforms, they selected faculty members from a wide cross-section of departments who were not necessarily the college's best teachers, but who believed in continuous improvement, were respected, were collaborative, and had positive attitudes. These professors, the administrators believed, would likely be successful with the new approaches, and would therefore serve as effective ambassadors for their broader adoption.

Larry Bigham, who has taught chemistry at West Kentucky since 1988, says that when learning outcomes were first introduced, he and his departmental colleagues saw them as merely "another set of forms we have to fill out on top of all the other forms we have to fill out. It was not well received." At another school, faculty may have complied with the mandate to the extent required, waiting for leaders to find another focus before putting aside the paperwork needed to assess learning.

But West Kentucky administrators made it clear that learning outcomes, and the assessment elements that would measure them, were here to stay, and they kept pointing back to the data about student failure as the reason why. They also made clear that faculty could voice disagreement, Bigham says, which actually made it easier to get faculty on board, since they felt like they were heard. In time, the naysayers became the outliers, and many retired. Bigham himself "decided not to be swept over by the wave," and embraced the reforms.

With strong and persistent leadership, reforms like those at West Kentucky can take hold. In large part, an evolution like this can happen because success begets success. At West Kentucky, the data convinced some faculty that there was a problem; others were convinced once they saw a *solution*, as reading skills and other outcomes began to improve quantitatively. "When you're able to show the faculty the data, not just the feel-good we-think-we're-wonderful things but the real numbers, then I think the faculty trusts you more when you're moving toward your next initiative," says Renea Akin, dean of institutional research, planning, and effectiveness.

Leveraging External Motivators to Accelerate Reform

In higher education generally, even when change is embraced by leaders, it can be slow to take hold. Decision making happens in decentralized ways: each academic unit is responsible for its curriculum, committees weigh in on most important decisions, and tenure systems and union contracts, where they exist, can impose rules that complicate implementation.

At West Kentucky, leaders used an external mandate to accelerate improvements in student learning by setting deadlines and goals across the entire college. In 2004, the Southern Association of Colleges and Schools began to require the colleges it accredited to create and implement a five-year plan—known as a *quality enhancement plan*, or QEP—to improve institutional processes aimed specifically at measuring, and most important elevating, student learning. This new mandate marked a shift for the accreditation council, whose process had previously focused more on inputs: what kind of degrees the faculty had, for example, or how many were part-time versus full-time.[12]

When accreditation neared and West Kentucky had to design a QEP, administrators seized the requirement to set deadlines for reform. The area of focus made itself clear. The first time the school administered the Educational Testing Service's Proficiency Profile, only 40 percent of West Kentucky students were capable of basic reading skills, compared to around 60 percent nationally. Before then, Akin says, "we really had no idea that academically our students were that far below the norm." Add to that data on developmental placements, success in gateway courses, and degree completion, and administrators came to what seemed to some at the time a simplistic conclusion: they needed to help students read better.

Faculty—a few at first, then nearly everyone as success spread—were trained in how to teach reading strategies regardless of their course subject. The college established *learning circles*, cross-departmental groups of fifteen to twenty professors who gave each other advice about which teaching techniques helped most, and students were surveyed as well. That combination of self-reflection and focus on the student experience is a hallmark of the school's newfound commitment to continuous improvement. Leaders had been working on improving institutional effectiveness for years, but only when it was part of the new accreditation process were they able to build the database that was required for longitudinal study of improvement.

While accreditation created a sense of urgency, West Kentucky President Barbara Veazey says, the reading program was never sold as something the school had to do to please accreditors. Instead, Veazey says, "we've always couched everything in terms of, 'This is what our students are going to need in order to graduate.'"

AN UNEASY FRONTIER: LEARNING OUTCOMES AND PERSONNEL DECISIONS

It's possible that many years into the implementation of outcomes-based processes, a new way of thinking becomes so embedded in the culture of a school that resistance virtually disappears. But for now, it's clear that at even the best community colleges, some professors' attitudes have not changed. And in private moments, leaders make clear that they expect some holdouts—faculty who will not adopt learning-centered teaching approaches, who will retire before they will change.

As a result, institutions on the path to culture change have grown more attentive on the front end to ensure that people coming into the institution are on board with the new approaches. During the hiring process, interviewers make clear to job candidates the expectations regarding assessing learning outcomes, collaborating, and being observed in the classroom, and take measure of their reactions. "That's our culture now," says Akin of West Kentucky. "That is what we do. And we don't want to be bringing on people who aren't going to participate in that process."

When teachers are hired at West Kentucky or Valencia, they know they are expected to work to improve their teaching. The training they get before classes start has been redesigned not just to get them acquainted with the institution's logistics and policies, as is typical at orientations, but to give them strategies to improve student learning. Both colleges connect new professors in cohorts, with advisers, to meet with each other throughout their first year and work on not just the traditional topics of classroom management and processes, but also the meat of instruction.

First-year professors at Valencia take a series of seven workshops on the school's essential competencies for instructors, which include assessment and learning-centered teaching practices. New faculty at West Kentucky, during a four-day seminar and then in monthly meetings throughout the year, learn how to conduct mini-assessments, write a good syllabus, and create interactive in-class activities that would engage students more than a PowerPoint presentation. "We spend a great deal of time discussing and demonstrating and showing what kind of teaching we're expecting," says Kevin Gericke, an economics professor who helps run the seminar. "We want to make sure that all of our faculty understand the standard . . . we expect them to reach."

Engaging the Growing Ranks of Adjunct Faculty

There is, of course, a limit to the impact of hiring and orientation efforts. Large and growing proportions of faculty are adjuncts— hired at the last minute or employed to teach just one or two classes.

Even when colleges implement practices like new training procedures, it remains a challenge to engage adjuncts. They often aren't required to attend faculty meetings, or to take part in designing learning outcomes or rubrics. Their orientations are generally abridged, to say the least.

In large numbers of community colleges, part-time instructors, whose annualized salaries add up to less than $40,000 a year with few (if any) benefits, make up the majority of the faculty. It's a higher percentage than at four-year colleges, and it is growing. For them, not only is tenure not a possibility, but job security typically isn't either. In most places, adjunct faculty don't get more money, or a full-time job, for meeting student outcome goals. So how can we expect them to be engaged in reform efforts?

At Valencia, adjuncts who participate in a certain amount of training qualify for an increase in status and pay. Valencia notifies adjunct faculty months before they have to teach a class, providing time for new instructors to be oriented before they step into a classroom. Perhaps most importantly, when full-time, tenure-track faculty positions become available, most are hired from the ranks of adjuncts. At West Kentucky, professional development is videotaped so that adjuncts can watch, if they choose. But there is a ways to go in ensuring that all faculty benefit from these promising practices to improve their teaching, and in turn student learning.

With budget pressures mounting, the ranks of adjunct faculty in community colleges will almost certainly continue to grow for the foreseeable future. For this reason, existing strategies for increasing adjunct engagement in improving learning outcomes need to be not only replicated, but improved upon as well.

Assessing Instructors

There is one threshold that most community colleges simply haven't crossed, even those like West Kentucky and Valencia where faculty regularly strive to improve their teaching practice and student learning outcomes. Specifically, community colleges do not typically use student outcome data to assess faculty.

In K–12 education, teacher evaluations are increasingly tied to the test scores of their students. In higher education, that's taboo. Even collecting data so that instructors can compare their outcomes to those of their peers, as the West Kentucky computer science instructors do, is rare. Tammy Potter, West Kentucky's dean of business and computer-related technologies, says that at first, professors were paranoid about being compared or punished based on the assessment results of their students. "I have worked very, very hard to make the point that this is not something that can be used against you," Potter says. "This is something to help you improve, something to help us move forward."

In many of the best K–12 schools, school principals pay close attention to the quantifiable results achieved by each teacher's students.[13] But few deans do this; many more go out of their way not to. Even when she is working to ensure that an adjunct instructor is not rehired, Potter will bring every bit of information to the table except learning outcomes data—no matter how clearly they make her case.

At Valencia, the action research projects and other learning outcomes work are required for and play a role in the tenure process, but actually improving student learning doesn't factor into the decision process. "We didn't want to taint that very supportive collegial experience," Helen Clarke says.

In many community colleges, as in other higher education institutions, professors are assessed through end-of-course student evaluations, which are sometimes used as a factor in tenure decisions. But professors are also valued differently in many community colleges based on the academic degree they hold or the number of years they have been teaching. In Florida, for example, many community colleges adhere to a pay schedule that provides step increases based on the different credentials and levels of seniority professors hold.

Research in the K–12 sector has found that while there are significant variances in the effectiveness of different teachers, there is little correlation between the results a teacher's students achieve and whether that teacher has earned an advanced degree.[14] Why would we expect it to be different in a higher education setting?

Yet community colleges rarely examine student outcomes by professor, acting as though student results will not vary much based on which professors teach which students in what courses. This is most easily justified at colleges with cultures of achievement, places where systemic improvements in teaching practice were built by professors deeply concerned about student success and where leaders support professors and challenge them to improve. After all, in K–12 schools with strong cultures, the greatest promise of new teacher evaluation systems is not how they are used to punish, but how they can be used to help teachers get better.

By understanding which teachers are achieving greater student learning gains, schools can identify "master teachers," who can become vital resources for colleagues seeking to improve. But without actually knowing whose teaching is most effective, it becomes hard to determine where to point struggling teachers for guidance.

In a recent conversation, a community college president described to me information he had discovered about professor effectiveness that could have a dramatic impact on student outcomes. Trying to figure out what could be changed to improve student success rates in developmental math—a serious challenge faced by most community colleges—the institution's senior team collected information about every variable that might be changed to reduce the high rate of student failure. One element stood out: student success varied dramatically based on instructor. Students in one instructor's developmental math course got an A, B, or C 75 percent of the time; students in another instructor's class did so only 18 percent of the time.

Worried about the implications of acting on this information—or even being thought by faculty to have done so—this president requested anonymity. The implication: a critical variable in student learning cannot even be discussed out of fear that doing so will alienate faculty, or result in a vote of "no confidence" for the president.

It is not simple to assess student learning in higher education. Community college students can pursue many possible degrees, and each offers innumerable combinations of courses that are either required or optional. Given such variability, it is hard to imagine a set of student learning outcomes, as has been pursued through the Common Core State Standards in the K–12 sector, that could be used to assess professors across all courses and programs.

Some researchers, however, have devised methods of assessing professor performance based on student outcomes, and have found significant variation using those methods. Specifically, professor quality can be measured by examining student performance both in a professor's course and in the next course in a sequence, and then comparing those outcomes with those of other professors. For example, if Professor A's students succeed in Psychology 101 more often than Professor B's students, and those students also do as well or better in Psychology 201, that suggests that Professor A has done a relatively good job not only retaining students but achieving quality in student learning as well.[15]

The current state of affairs, however, prevents colleges and instructors from gaining critical insights into what makes some teachers better than others—information that could be used to help all instructors serve students better. Surely, a professor whose students succeed 18 percent of the time can learn *something* important from a professor whose students succeed more than four times as often. But that learning will rarely, if ever, happen if no one knows which professor achieved which outcomes.

Some might ask whether colleges even need to identify exceptional teachers. After all, Valencia and West Kentucky do not routinely use learning outcomes results to identify the most (or least) effective professors, yet they have developed cultures of excellence, built around efforts to develop learning-centered colleges. Indeed, they prove that much can be accomplished by building expectations and training into the hiring and tenure processes, by sharing data on student outcomes across departments, and by creating the time and space for faculty to improve their craft—individually and together.

But even excellent community colleges have a long way to go. Nearly every community college is still struggling to achieve strong results for many students—most notably those who enter college needing significant developmental education. To address this and other persistent student success challenges, even the best community colleges may find it necessary to determine which professors deliver the most effective education, so the entire college can figure out how to do the same.

At other, lower performing community colleges, evaluations may need to be used for other purposes. In some schools, faculty are suspicious of leaders, and suggested changes in practice are met with deep resistance and routinely picked apart in collective bargaining, regardless of whether they hold promise to improve poor outcomes for students. In these especially difficult circumstances, it is worth considering whether holding professors accountable for student results would be an important way to improve student outcomes, with termination among the possible consequences for low performers.

In the end, community college leaders, policy makers, and others who care about improving community college student success should consider how current systems and dynamics enable every community college professor to truly understand what great teaching looks like. Moving closer to that goal will allow professional development, tenure, and other human resources systems to be aligned in ways that ensure that more students learn at a high level.

Quantifying Learning

How can community colleges compare the amount students learn across programs as varied as philosophy and welding? Even in the few fields that have common end-of-program assessments, such as nursing, how can states and systems measure how much students learn at different colleges in a way that accounts for the different preparation levels students may have arrived with?

Other recent efforts confirm how hard it is to gather comparative measures of learning outcomes. In 2012, the American Association of Community Colleges released its Voluntary Framework of Account-ability, which aimed to go beyond graduation rates as the primary measure of a school's success. The list included seventeen measures for assessing completion outcomes—for example, by measuring the percentage of students who made it through developmental classes, or who were retained from one term to the next. Ten metrics were listed to indicate how well a school was contributing to work force and economic development. But when it came to learning outcomes, the document said only that colleges need to be more transparent in how they assess student learning outcomes. No metrics were included.

Over the prior decade, the National Center for Public Policy and Higher Education had much the same problem when developing a state-by-state report card. Its first assessment, called *Measuring Up 2000*, gave an "incomplete" to every state in the category of college student learning, "because there are no common benchmarks that would allow meaningful state-to-state comparisons."[16] Six years later, *Measuring Up 2006* reported that nine states deserved recognition, not for making measurable gains in student learning, but for adopt-ing certain measurement tools and systems.[17] Comparative metrics for learning were still not available.

This is not to say that learning in community colleges can never be measured quantitatively and compared across campuses. Programs that require licensure—such as in certain computer science competencies or nursing and other health programs—generally culminate in common end-of-program exams. Similarly, schools routinely use standardized tests to assess students' readiness for college-level work, and some use those same tests as exit exams to measure whether students have mastered remedial coursework. But these are exceptions; a very limited number of community college courses and programs use learning assessment tools that are common across institutions.

That may be changing, though. More and more higher education content is being delivered via technology, largely driven by the desire to cut costs, expand access, and, for increasing numbers of educators, make a profit. Online classes offer computer assessments that enable much more information about student learning to be captured, stored, and shared. Already, thousands of students are taking common assessments in *massively open online courses*, known as MOOCs, from providers that include Harvard, the Massachusetts Institute of Technology, Stanford, and other elite colleges. The extent to which technology pushes higher education toward common curricula and assessments—delivered by different professors at different institutions—will determine, in large part, how much comparative analysis of learning will be possible.

While professors' roles may change as technology advances, it is hard to imagine that they will (or should) lose their important place in the delivery of education anytime soon. So the best colleges must continue to devise systems that not only assess whether students are learning at the course level, the program level, and institution-wide, but also make sure that professors use those assessments to figure out how to close gaps in learning and then measure whether those improvements work.

4

LABOR MARKETS

Tying Learning and Credentials to Jobs and Community

IMAGINE LIVING IN AN IMPOVERISHED area with few job opportunities. You've just graduated high school, or been laid off from a job. Or maybe you live in a thriving city, but you don't quite have what it takes to afford or gain entrance to a selective four-year college. Nobody in your family has gone on to higher education, but you know that in order to make something of yourself, you'll have to. So you enroll at the local community college.

For some people, this pays off: the schooling leads to a great career, either directly or by way of a four-year college. But for every community college graduate who ends up with a $40,000 or $50,000 job as a petrochemical technician right after graduating, another earns $15,000 as a massage therapist.

There is a huge discrepancy among community colleges, and programs within them, when it comes to labor market outcomes. Some colleges' graduates far outearn other new hires in their region, while others earn little more than high school graduates.

Likewise, job placement rates vary widely. With millions of Americans relying on community colleges to jump-start their future, how can schools make sure that leap of faith pays off?

Left to themselves, community college students often have little clarity about what programs and courses will bring them success. So leaders and staff at excellent community colleges know that it is up to them to do everything they can to ensure that what students learn and the credentials they complete lead to jobs that offer not just strong wages but room for growth. They shut or retool programs that don't deliver; they start and grow ones that do. They nimbly respond to industry needs, in both what they teach and how. They provide students the information required to make smart choices.

The most innovative colleges don't stop there. When the regions they serve don't offer the kind of jobs they know their graduates deserve, they do nothing short of helping to resuscitate the local economy to create opportunity, for graduates and for the community at large.

OFFERING THE RIGHT PROGRAMS

A college that wants to ensure strong job prospects for graduates must first align its degree programs with projections of what jobs will be available, with decent wages, when students graduate. Often working with vendors or state systems with access to data from the U.S. Department of Labor and other sources, strong community colleges assess trends in job growth and salaries to determine the degrees that will be needed for high-demand jobs that are likely to offer good wages. They then structure their programs and enrollment in accordance with those demands.

Especially in a rapidly changing economy, such projections can never be 100 percent accurate. So effective community college leaders don't just look at the data; they talk about where the economy might be headed with the people who know best: employers. If the data show that graduates' wages are increasing, employers can distinguish whether that is likely to continue or an anomaly. And if some jobs in a sector are drying up, employers can help the college see trends in the field—new technologies coming online, promising new products being developed—to suggest what programs might be created or expanded to offer new opportunities for graduates.

But it is not enough to align programs with projected job openings. Even when good jobs materialize, graduates will be out of luck if colleges do not equip them with skills that employers actually want. Colleges need to look at what actually happens to students after they graduate.

You might assume colleges would already be using all the information at their disposal to make programmatic decisions that are singularly focused on increasing graduates' chances for success. In actuality, though, many forces drive decision makers to consider other factors that influence their choices.

At most U.S. colleges, decisions about what programs are offered and required are made through processes that include committees of faculty working with the department chairs and deans in their disciplines. While some of them have employment trend data in hand when making such decisions, faculty members also have their own preferences, which sometimes trump other considerations.

In one sense, it may be helpful to take faculty preferences into consideration. After all, faculty who are passionate about and expert in a subject are, all else equal, more likely to be engaging and productive professors than those assigned to teach something they don't care or know much about. This process, though, can fail to serve students, when the programs that faculty members want to pursue or sustain don't line up with the skills required for available good jobs. And faculty sometimes don't have current knowledge of what those skills are.

Also, high costs can be a deterrent to expanding programs in high-demand, high-wage fields. Nursing and other health care programs at community colleges, for example, routinely have long waiting lists and plenty of good jobs awaiting graduates. Yet colleges sometimes limit enrollment because of the high cost of delivering those programs (which is mostly driven by relatively small classes and expensive equipment).

Excellent community colleges don't let these constraints limit them. By examining data and maintaining strong relationships with employers, they understand what students need to get jobs. They act swiftly to do whatever is needed—from program design to resource allocation—to align their programs accordingly.

Opening and Closing Programs

Steven VanAusdle, the longtime president of Walla Walla Community College, grew up in eastern Washington. When its agriculture-based economy started to falter in the mid-1990s—automation claimed some jobs, and others moved abroad—he felt a profound sense of urgency, for his students and for his community. VanAusdle, who was trained as a labor economist, spent the next decade and a half reconfiguring the college to maximize the chances that students will land good jobs, a process that never ends.

One example: tall, white wind turbines generating clean electricity began to bloom in the area, symbols of technological innovation in an otherwise agrarian economy. Some might see beauty in the windmills. Others might see horizon destroyers. What does VanAusdle see? A future for graduates. He got the state's first college wind energy program up and running. "We've invested, in a very tough economy, $5 million in the program," he says. "We are going to scale it, because the jobs are there." And students are the clear winners: 71 percent complete the program, 90 percent are placed in jobs with starting salaries over $37,000 per year, and most earn overtime.

Walla Walla also shuts programs down. It closed its culinary program when data showed that graduates were getting only low-wage food service jobs. (The program was reopened a few years later to respond to growing tourism demands and retooled to train students in higher-wage jobs, like catering.) Carpentry was closed too, even though enrollment numbers were strong, because jobs were drying up along with housing construction. Similarly, Lake Area Technical Institute had lots of interest in a large-animal veterinary program, but because a market analysis showed that the jobs weren't there, the idea never got off the ground.

Adding and Subtracting Seats

Community colleges that align program decisions to employment opportunities don't do so just when opening and closing programs; they routinely adjust enrollment in the programs based on work force need. In the late 1990s, Walla Walla college leaders knew their nursing graduates were getting good jobs. They looked at the data and saw that the four hospitals in the region could absorb twice as many nurses as the school was producing. So Walla

Walla doubled the size of its nursing program, also adding more science instructors to beef up pre-nursing courses so more students were well prepared.

This was an expensive move. But at Walla Walla, dollars are allocated for what matters most. Closing unsuccessful programs (no matter how popular) makes it possible to expand successful ones. And when local funds are not enough, the college aggressively seeks state and private funds. For example, VanAusdle, whose students posted strong board exam pass rates, got the state to provide higher per-student funding for nursing than for other programs.

Sometimes data indicate that a program is still necessary for the region but doesn't need to be as big as it is. For years, Cabrillo College, located outside Santa Cruz, California, graduated medical assistants into a labor market with, it seemed, plenty of jobs in the field.[1] Yet Cabrillo graduates had relatively low employment rates. Deeper investigation revealed a market oversaturated with graduates from area community college programs, none of which alone could meet labor market demands but which together produced too many graduates. The college is reducing the medical assistant program to two-thirds the size it once was.

These may sound like obvious decisions. After all, why would a college maintain seats in a program—or even offer a program at all—that is, in essence, a road to nowhere? Because many incentives pull it in the opposite direction.

Historically, community colleges have been rewarded for enrolling students. For every student enrolled in a course, a college receives tuition, state higher education allocations tied to individual students, and federal and state financial aid dollars, including Pell Grants for needy students—whether or not that class leads students to success. That incentive system has produced predictable results. If students are willing to enroll in a course or a program, many colleges are likely to offer it.

To some extent, student demand corrects for such mismatches. Nursing programs, for example, remain in high demand in many places because jobs are relatively plentiful and well paying. And programs that clearly don't offer students quality training are bound to lose enrollment over time and, if they don't improve, get shut down.

But, for several reasons, the laws of the market don't work very well on community college campuses. Students are often not provided good information about employment and earnings rates for graduates with various credentials, and the places where students can find that information on their own are few and far between. So many students remain undecided, struggling to figure out what they want to study for a year or two after arriving on campus. Given the average time it takes community college students who start full-time to earn a credential—3.8 years for a two-year degree—it should come as no surprise that students wander through the curriculum, sometimes taking courses that don't align to valuable degrees at all.[2]

HELPING STUDENTS MAKE THE RIGHT CHOICES

Excellent colleges do what they can to lead students to the smartest possible decisions. They don't just post information about job and wage prospects on a Web site, they show it to students at every opportunity. They train advisers to walk students through pathways, letting students know which courses and programs will prepare them for which futures (and what those futures look like). And, in certain cases, they narrow choices for students so it is much harder to make a bad one.

Informing Students About Outcomes

In June 2012, the Community College Research Center at Columbia University revealed some startling findings. Ten years after graduating, women who had received a two-year degree in the humanities from a Washington State community college earned only 5 percent more than those with just a high school degree. Women who got a nursing degree, though, earned 37 percent more than high school graduates.[3] A recent report showed similar disparities for recent community college graduates in Tennessee: graduates in the health professions had an average salary of $47,000, compared to less than $26,000 for graduates in education.[4]

Students often have no idea what opportunities are available to them. Knowing this, community colleges are beginning to experiment with helping students make better decisions. Many schools think it is enough to give students "What Color Is Your Parachute?"–type quizzes to match their personalities to professions. But the most effective colleges know that no matter how well suited a student is to a career, it does not matter if she'll never get a job. These schools counsel students not just on fit but also on opportunity.

At Walla Walla, students must see an adviser before registering each quarter, and many report leaving those meetings with detailed printouts of each career they're considering, the job and wage prospects in that field, and the courses required for the degree. Colleges can also deliver this information through online tools—which work best when steps are taken to make sure students use them. Monroe Community College in Rochester, New

York, has an easy-to-use, Web-based tool that indicates which career and technical programs lead to local hiring opportunities and strong wages, and it puts this tool in front of students before they even enroll. The city school district identifies people who are ready for and interested in college, including high school students and unemployed adults, and Monroe provides them a free course that uses the tool to help them select a career with good potential—one they may never even have known about.

Deciding Between Colleges

These approaches are helpful for students deciding what to study. But what about those deciding which college to attend? Very few Americans base their decision on where to go to college on how likely graduates are to be employed and how much they will earn after graduating from a specific college with a specific degree. How could they? How does a consumer figure out whether the investment of time and money is better spent in one particular community college program than another?

It is clear that students often make uninformed choices. Research has shown that colleges with similar student bodies and resources often have radically different degree completion rates, yet students still choose schools that are unlikely to lead them to degrees.[5] The federal and several state governments are currently working to make better consumer information available about college costs and outcomes, hoping to improve students' chances of success and economic prospects, and in turn drive changes in how colleges operate.

Of course, the idea of using labor market outcomes to inform student choice might not be welcomed by most community colleges, for fear that doing so might curtail enrollment in programs with poor outcomes for graduates. But if their leaders truly care first and foremost about student success, they should embrace this flow of information.

TEACHING THE RIGHT THINGS

When Cabrillo College leaders examined why students in their medical assistant program were not getting jobs, they had to look beyond labor market databases to find the full answer. They held a meeting with twenty local employers, who informed them that Cabrillo graduates were not reaching the high standards required in the field. In addition to shrinking the program, the leaders beefed up English and math skills instruction for the students who remained.[6]

Good colleges know this kind of communication is crucial if they want their students not just to get hired but to succeed in their jobs. Through close relationships with employers, colleges learn what skills, both technical and interpersonal, their students need and how to deliver instruction in ways that reflect what will be expected on the job.

It is common for technical programs at community colleges to have advisory boards, which gather employers from the region to advise faculty and deans. Sometimes those boards are built mainly on easygoing social relationships between educators and the industry. While a few meetings a year can always help identify important developments—say, the speed at which dental hygiene is moving from film to digital imaging—understanding how well community college programs actually train students for jobs takes much more.

Exceptional colleges use advisory board members, and anyone else they can get in touch with, as a weekly (if not daily) resource to learn about trends in the industry, hear about how graduates are doing, connect students with field experiences, and provide materials and equipment so that students can walk out with their diplomas ready to work on day one. These boards work best when they serve not just as trusted partners but also as constructive critics.

"In my early career I was a program coordinator, and I recognized what a challenge it was to have business involvement in your program and how you gravitate to those employers who are always saying what you want to hear," recalls West Kentucky's Barbara Veazey. As president, she makes sure programs hear what they need, not just what they want. When programs are stagnating, new advisory board members are added. And programs are put through whatever accreditation process is available—and re-accreditation—even if not required for funding.

A Never-Ending Cycle of Change

For a very long time, the most important machine on a farm—a tractor—had been relatively simple for farmers to use and repair. But starting in the late twentieth century, automation and computerization brought a radically different set of skills to the profession. Today's new tractors can be operated remotely and are directed by more than fifty separate on-board computers. Using and fixing these tractors requires skills no longer easily passed on from parent to child.

Seeing this, Walla Walla overhauled its tractor mechanic program, which it runs in collaboration with John Deere. Once trained on lifts and engines, students now focus on computerized diagnostic instruments. Once trained to diagnose problems by examining equipment on site—often resulting in multiple hours-long trips to a farm before a tractor was fixed—students now learn how to counsel farmers to plug a computer into their tractor and send information to the dealership so that workers can fix problems remotely or, if they have to go to the farm, can arrive with the right parts in hand.

If this sounds harder than fixing an engine the old-fashioned way, it is. "I've always done very well in school my whole life," says student Mike Cain, who used to fix recreational vehicles before the 2008 recession reduced the need for RV mechanics. "Here, I am fighting—working really, really hard—to maintain a B average. I can't believe how sophisticated the training here is."

At good community colleges, technical programs—from airplane mechanics to welding to computer numeric controls—adapt each term to the ever-changing needs of industry. That kind of perpetual progress is made possible by instructors who are both flexible enough to change course quickly and engaged with employers enough to know when they need to.

Delivering Hands-On Education

Officials from Walla Walla's conservation district had a problem to fix: farmers had placed water pumps in the streams with no screens on them, so fish were being sucked in and were dying in the fields. There were funds to address the issue, but nobody to do the job; relations between farmers and environmentalists in the area were fraught, and people were wary of entering the fray. The irrigation technology instructors at Walla Walla, however, had no such compunctions. They saw this as a way to get students engaged in a real-world problem that could teach them practical skills in a context that mattered to their local community.

Research revealed to students that nobody manufactured a screen that met state regulations. So they designed one, found a company to manufacture it, and installed the first ten as a test. When the screens worked, the conservation district contracted out the installation of hundreds more. Today, there are more than eight hundred screens in place on farms throughout the region.

This was a real-life problem to solve that felt relevant to students. Textbook learning can be frustrating for students eager to work in the field; exceptional colleges understand this and make sure that their technical programs are challenging and engaging—real practice for what graduates will be expected to do on the job.

This kind of education often requires state-of-the-art equipment. Walla Walla plans to build a wind turbine at the state penitentiary, both to meet a community need and give its students a practice facility. At Lake Area Technical Institute, in a mammoth, vehicle-packed facility, aspiring diesel technicians get to use the only truck chassis dynamometer at a South Dakota school so they can learn to measure the force of an engine, a critical skill. Students learning to be airplane mechanics there work on Cessnas and Beechcrafts and even a 727, not just simulated electrical systems or ancient engines pulled from a scrap heap.

How do colleges afford this equipment? It helps to educate students so well that local businesses rely on colleges for talented graduates. The petrochemical companies near Brazosport College, most notably Dow Chemical and BASF, employ a steady stream of process technology graduates, so they funded college labs equipped with the same technologies and control systems used in the field, including a full-size glycol distillation plant. Dow has so much confidence in the equipment and teaching at Brazosport that it sends its own hires to be trained at the college, in a fourteen-week program. There, the cycle continues, as Dow representatives continue to inform the college instructors, providing feedback on site "on a day-to-day basis," says Gary Hicks, chair of the process technology division and a former Dow employee.

Instilling Interpersonal Skills

In Walla Walla's energy systems program, students are called "employees." Homework is called "work assignments." "We treat this place like a job every day from the very beginning," says James Bradshaw, the program director.

Leading community college students into careers is not just about giving them content knowledge and technical skills. Often, they need to be taught to be employees. When college instructors communicate with businesses, they often hear that their students know their stuff but lack *soft skills*: how to communicate effectively, work with others, manage conflict, and present oneself.

So, many professors set expectations like an employer would. Students are penalized if they are late or absent. They are required to dress as they would have to on the job. Failing to complete assignments is treated just like failing to complete tasks at work. Bradshaw's students want him to recommend them for jobs, and he tells them that their work ethic has to be impeccable for him to do so. They may never have faced such expectations before. "For many who we chastise," Bradshaw says, "it helps turn their lives around."

AN ECONOMY TRANSFORMED

In the early 1990s, downtown Walla Walla "looked like it had been bombed out. Everything was boarded up," says Myles Anderson, a longtime professor at the college. A few predictable rural town establishments persisted: a diner, a pharmacy, the five-and-dime.

There wasn't much else to speak of, except for a cattle drive that ran down Main Street, through tumbleweed.

Today, downtown Walla Walla has been reinvented into something else altogether: a vibrant tourist town where affluent Pacific Northwesterners go to celebrate fortieth birthdays and thirtieth anniversaries, where foodies track down meals written up in *Sunset* magazine and, first and foremost, drink wine. The town's most prominent features today are dozens of tasting rooms, where tourists flock to sample the area's award-winning wines. In the late 1990s, there were seven operating vineyards among the hayfields of the Walla Walla Valley. Today, high rows of grapevines and steel prefabricated winemaking buildings are impossible to miss—there were 170 wineries at last count. The sense of despair that once marked the region, as the agriculture work around which many had built their lives became less reliable, has given way to a climate of robust employment opportunity and potential.

Typically community colleges respond to local economic needs. Walla Walla Community College, on the other hand, has managed to help create the economy itself, by starting a grape growing and winemaking degree program that is credited with feeding the growth of the industry. "Across America, rural towns in the 1990s were in deep trouble," recalls longtime resident and winemaker Marty Clubb. "A lot of things came together in Walla Walla to change that, and the community college was a big part of that."

Winemaking isn't a natural fit for a college—especially one in a conservative community. State politicians didn't like the idea of alcohol being made on a college campus, and local winemakers feared competition from the working college winery. But now that resistance is ancient history, as the region enjoys the carryover effect of the industry's success (and as the local winemakers have come to rely on Walla Walla graduates). A thousand acres of vineyard, according to a 2009 analysis done for the college, translates into three hundred jobs, over $10 million in earnings, and about $70 million in wine sales. But the impact doesn't stop there. The college has reconceived its culinary program based on the new catering demands of a tourist economy, trains students in wine photography, and offers a sommelier certificate. Railex, a refrigerated rail service, just opened a $20 million, 500,000-square-foot storage facility nearby to store 5 million cases of wine for transporting across the country.

The economic transformation shows just how central a community college can be in changing labor market conditions. It shows how innovative college leaders see their college's health and the community's health as inextricably linked, and act to improve both. Graduates of the enology and viticulture program will get jobs, of course, but so will the college's surveyors, nurses, auto mechanics, chefs, golf course managers, and welders—because they will be graduating into a healthy economy.

The wine program is part of a bigger effort by the college to innovate in sustainable industries. ("Growing grapes takes a lot less water than growing alfalfa or irrigated wheat," says Jim Peterson, the college's vice president for administrative services.) Forty-five minutes away, on the Confederated Tribes of the Umatilla Indian Reservation, salmon, a core cultural and religious symbol for the tribe members, have been coming back to the river in growing numbers, after seventy years of absence. While nobody would credit the community college alone for the salmon's return, the role the college plays—providing a permanent center for and being part of conversations about what to do next in watershed restoration—reflects the vision of the president. "For too long, we have grown our economy by taking from the environment in unsustainable ways," VanAusdle says. "What we are building here will last, because it is sustainable."

The college is also "doubling down on renewable energy," as VanAusdle puts it. "That is the future." It spent nearly $300,000 recently to build a classroom to train wind energy students in programmable logical controls. A new certificate in alternative fuels is being added to the automotive programs. Students are participating in a grant to convert poplar trees into jet fuel. A program whereby the college purchases vehicles with collision damage and has students fix them up for sale to state offices now specializes in hybrid cars.

"It used to be that when wheat prices were up, we were all doing great. When they bottomed out, it was a disaster," VanAusdle says. "We were such a vulnerable community. Compare that to now. During the recent recession, there was no stasis. There was continued growth."

Not every community college has access to the assets Walla Walla does: open space, a climate that welcomes winemaking, and reasonable proximity to wealthy cities. But all effective community college leaders understand that the best their community has to offer now—and could develop in the future—is too often out of reach for many of the students their community college educates. Exceptional community colleges develop that link, providing students the specific skills they need to access good jobs, helping employers grow even more opportunity, and constantly checking to make sure that dreams and expectations are fulfilled.

A NOTE ON MEASUREMENT

Labor Market Outcomes

Many community colleges use labor market data to analyze whether their programs are aligned with projected needs in their local communities and regions. Accessing data mostly from the U.S. Bureau of Labor Statistics and the Census Bureau, leaders of institutions and sometimes systems and states work to ensure that community colleges offer the right mix of manufacturing, allied health, and other credentials to ensure job opportunities and regional economic growth.[7]

While data that project into the future are essential to making decisions from year to year about what to offer, they have some significant limitations. With job requirements changing ever more rapidly in an age of technological advancement, projections may be less and less likely to match future realities. Even if students graduate from programs that are aligned with future labor market demand, they still may not get jobs if their training does not confer the skills they need to be hired into or remain in those jobs. So colleges are increasingly demanding information about how often students are actually employed and how much they earn after they graduate from each program.

For decades, community colleges have tracked and reported job outcomes for graduates of career and technical education programs, largely because doing so is required for some federal grants and, often, program accreditation. When a program's job placement rates fall to levels that might threaten accreditation or funding, colleges act to improve those programs. Those data, however, are often unreliable. Typically, colleges rely on surveys of graduates, who often choose not to respond.[8]

Moreover, requirements to report labor market outcomes don't apply to general education programs, so community colleges typically don't collect employment and earnings information on students who complete a degree unless it's tied to a specific career. Administrators sometimes want the information, and may even collect it quietly. But making it part of the public decision-making process is risky, as liberal arts professors often resist the idea that employment and earnings should be measured or directly linked to what they are teaching.

Today, there is a growing amount of reliable labor market data available on all community college graduates. Over half of states today have systems (or will very soon) that match employment data—long used to administer unemployment insurance programs—with records of college graduates. And some are now publicly reporting employment and wage data of graduates not only by college but by major and program as well.[9] Many states have increased the accuracy of their employment data by sharing unemployment insurance records with neighboring states so they can track graduates who move across state lines. And in 2012, the U.S. Department of Education released "gainful employment" reports, which contained job placement rates for thousands of vocational programs at more than one thousand institutions, including community colleges.[10]

The emergence of these new data sets gives colleges a great tool to measure and improve student success. When effective community college leaders see from them that a program needs to be improved, they engage with employers and others in their communities, regularly and deeply, to figure out why. If graduates aren't getting jobs, employers can help these college leaders understand the reasons so that programs can be improved.

Employment and earnings data tied to colleges is still in the early stages of development. Among the important limitations (some of which will be sorted out in the coming decade):

- *Deciding how long after graduation to track students.* Employment and earnings information released in recent years has focused largely on outcomes in the year after students graduate. This almost certainly reveals relatively high employment and earnings rates for graduates of programs that are aligned with specific jobs, such as nursing, engineering, or welding. Graduates of liberal arts programs, however, may not land well-paying jobs for years after completing their degrees, either because it takes them more time to figure out how to apply their broader skills to a particular profession or because they are attending graduate school. It does not make much sense to compare the employment rates and wages during the year after graduation between a community college's auto mechanic program, which sends most graduates immediately into full-time jobs, and its political science program, from which far greater numbers of students transfer to a four-year college (and may attend graduate school after that). If numbers showed much better outcomes for the automotive students, it could be inferred that the mechanics with jobs are the best of the graduates, while the political science majors who started working right away (and thus did not transfer) were the program's weakest graduates. A complete picture of labor market outcomes requires analyzing wage data of graduates both one year and five or ten years after students graduate.

- *Assigning credit when students attend multiple institutions or receive multiple degrees.* For employment and wage information to have value, it must be able to be ascribed to the outcomes of particular programs and institutions. But, every year, increasing numbers of students pursue a single degree while attending different institutions. As technological delivery options expand and institutions become more willing to award credits to students who prove competency based on previous learning and experience (rather than based on clocking seat time), the number of possible pathways to a degree will grow, making it harder to figure out the value of any one pathway, let alone explain it to students, families, colleges, and policy makers. Similarly, consider a student who receives an associate's degree from a community college, and then goes on to get a bachelor's degree and a graduate degree at two other institutions. Which program is responsible for which part of that student's employment and wages after finishing school? Analytically, these issues can be sorted out, but making meaning in the face of such variation will become increasingly hard.

- *Accounting for students who move between states.* Much of the work being done to assess employment and wage outcomes for college graduates happens at the state level, utilizing wage records in systems created to provide state worker unemployment insurance. Because these data sets are contained in single-state systems, they fail to include graduates who move across state lines. They also fail to capture members of the military or self-employed workers. In 2013, U.S. Senators Marco Rubio (a Florida Republican) and Ron Wyden (an Oregon Democrat) introduced a bill that would effectively eliminate both the interstate mobility and limited coverage problems by creating a federal student unit record system that would allow for the collection of information on all graduates' wages using federal data. But the prospects of passage appear limited, leaving colleges with useful but imperfect labor market data with which to assess student outcomes.

5

THE COMMUNITY
COLLEGE PRESIDENT

Driving to Excellence in a
Fast-Changing Environment

I N 2002, TWO LONGTIME INSTITUTIONS—one academic community college and one technical school—merged to become West Kentucky Community and Technical College. Barbara Veazey, the new president, had come through the community college, where she had been dean of nursing. The technical school, she'd always heard, was one of the nation's best.

Except that it wasn't. During her first months on the job, Veazey spent time in the technical programs and visited those at other schools. She could easily tell that the West Kentucky programs—the teaching, the equipment—fell short, and that students weren't being prepared well for good jobs. An economic development official who had moved to Paducah from a high-tech region toured the campus and delivered a blunt assessment: "Oh, Barbara," he said, "my garage looks better than this."

The instinct of many leaders might have been to write off that assessment as too harsh, to decry such criticism as insensitive to the context in which community colleges operate. Even leaders who know their institutions have problems can be paralyzed by what they see as limited resources or constraints in their authority to mandate change. In any event, few would make their shortcomings public.

Veazey, though, was determined to confront serious problems head-on. She led a series of trips so that a group of civic and business leaders, faculty, and staff could see firsthand colleges that were recognized for excellence, attracted major employers, and achieved better results for students. With the support of her governing board, Veazey aggressively pursued an audacious goal: to make West Kentucky a premier community college like the ones they visited, not just regionally but nationally.

"I went through several of these conversations with my colleagues, other presidents, who thought . . . that was too lofty of a goal," Veazey says. "How could you ever measure it? And how could you ever achieve it on our paltry budget that we had in Kentucky?" Faculty and deans, too, were wary. "Premier," they said, was unattainable. Couldn't she choose a different word?

A decade later, West Kentucky Community and Technical College is indeed a premier institution, ranked in the top ten in each of the first two years of the Aspen Prize competition. That kind of improvement doesn't come easily, of course. Veazey talks of "getting the right people on the bus," which of course means showing others the exit. She confronted her entire college with institution-wide reading scores that were significantly lower than the national average, challenging faculty to solve the problem. She worked her way to the presidency of the local chamber of commerce board, ensuring that the college did whatever was needed to fuel economic growth in the area, whether that be a new riverboat technician program or an art school. In these and other ways, Veazey has done what exceptional community college presidents do: aim not just to change practices and habits but to build new values and attitudes as well. That hardly ever happens without a strong, enterprising leader at the helm—someone who is honest about an institution's weaknesses and relentless in the drive to improve them.

THE PRESIDENCY AT A TIME OF CHANGE

Within the next five years, 43 percent of all community college presidents are expected to retire.[1] This reflects the reality of the job; for some time, the median tenure for a community college presidency has been short—five years (compared to ten in the 1980s). But the coming turnover represents something more: the aging of community college presidents. According to the American Association of Community Colleges, the average age of community college presidents increased from fifty-one in 1986 to fifty-seven in 1998, and it is now around sixty.[2]

Given the resources it takes to fill these jobs and the upheaval that turnover creates, some might view this impending mass of retirements as a crisis. It makes more sense to view it as an opportunity.[3] After all, the world of community colleges is changing, and growing ever more challenging.

The biggest change: colleges are beginning to be held accountable for student results. Federal and state governments are increasingly requiring community colleges to report completion, employment, and earnings outcomes for their students, and many states are tying funding to these outcomes, rather than simply allocating money based on how many students enroll. Policy makers in both parties have begun to insist that information about student outcomes be made easily available to the public.[4] And a wide variety of leaders—starting with President Obama—have called on colleges to graduate more students.

For today's community colleges, though, the changes are not just about new expectations for outcomes but new ways to meet them. Technology now allows for ways of delivering instruction that do not require students to sit in a classroom before a professor. While this offers community colleges the chance to become much more efficient (and potentially more effective), taking full advantage of this opportunity requires college leaders who can re-envision many of their institutions' basic functions: does being a professor require developing curriculum, instructing students, *and* assessing student learning? Does technology allow some kinds of courses to be delivered more effectively and efficiently by outside providers? What portion of a degree can students earn through technologically assessed competencies, whether or not that material was learned in traditional courses?

Driven in part by these technological advances, there is an explosion in the competition for students traditionally served by community colleges. New schools, many of them for-profit endeavors, bring substantial investment capital, well-developed marketing strategies, and new ways of thinking about educational delivery.[5] Unencumbered by tradition, these schools are reinventing faculty roles, measurement of student learning, and program structures and schedules in ways that are not so easy for traditional community colleges to emulate.

For their survival, to say nothing of their students' chances for success, community colleges will have to adapt to these rapid technological changes and increased expectations. At the same time, community college students will continue to enroll with significant disadvantages: jobs to make time for, remedial needs to overcome, children to raise. What it's taken to achieve good student outcomes in the past is not the same as what it will take to achieve good outcomes—much less great ones—in the future. Likewise, what it took for yesterday's community college president to be effective may not be enough for tomorrow's.

It is imperative that we seize the opportunity provided by the impending turnover of so many leaders. All people charged with training or hiring future community college presidents must keep a sharp focus on improving student success. They need to understand that effective leadership is borne not just from charisma or a certain résumé, but also from taking risks and changing cultures in ways that align to student success goals. They should look to the examples of exceptional community college presidents—those who have led institutions to dramatically improved student outcomes—to identify the qualities that will enable future leaders to experience the same level of success in a rapidly changing world.[6]

CREATING URGENCY FOR SUCCESS BY OWNING FAILURE

When the economic development official told Barbara Veazey that West Kentucky was not equipped to draw businesses to the area, she didn't contradict him—she had him repeat the message to the board of trustees and invited local business leaders to tour the college's lackluster training facilities with a reporter in tow. When Robert Templin at Northern Virginia Community College announced to dozens of colleagues recently that his institution had improved graduation rates from 12 percent to 20 percent during his eight-year tenure, he quickly followed by saying, "That means that four out of five students don't succeed. That is unacceptable." For Kenneth Ender, the president of Harper College outside of Chicago, that his college has a graduation and transfer rate 10 percentage points above the national average is not enough. "He made clear that we had to keep looking at the data until we came up with a specific target for a graduation rate that would ensure that Harper does its part to meet Illinois's graduation goal," recalls Sheila Quirk, a vice president at the college.

It may seem counterintuitive: who wants to run the risk of damaging morale by broadcasting how badly the college has been doing? Indeed, when Ender suggested to fellow community college presidents in a recent meeting that every college should publicly acknowledge current graduation rates and then "name a number"—set a target for graduation rates—another community college leader replied, "No one wants to be embarrassed."

But strong leaders understand that creating urgency sometimes means risking embarrassment. Presidents who have achieved excellence for students started by making clear—honestly and often—just how inadequate results are for students. They show the data, again and again, in hopes of building consensus for change. They take ownership of the college's shortcomings and don't blame others. They persistently communicate the message to stakeholders inside and outside the college: our students deserve better.

Professors and administrators at a college may not know that only half the students who start its remedial sequence complete it (as was the case at Broward College in Fort Lauderdale, Florida, before the new president started publicizing outcomes data). They may not know that only 40 percent of students have basic reading skills (as had been the case at West Kentucky). Once they are made aware, it's hard for them to deny that things must change—that *they* must change.

But change takes time, often longer than the typical president's five-year tenure. U.S. colleges and universities have common cultural elements that have been developing, and hardening, since the institutions were first created in the eighteenth century.[7] While community colleges are much newer, the same forces—disciplinary specialty, faculty autonomy, a semester-based course structure—make them equally difficult to move.

It is not a surprise, then, that at the top colleges honored in the Aspen Prize competition—institutions where change has taken hold—the average tenure for presidents is more than ten years. At colleges where student success is at a standstill, that might be many years too long. At colleges with improving outcomes, that longevity is critical.

Keeping presidents capable of leading community colleges to high and improving levels of success may become increasingly hard in an era of accountability. When Steven VanAusdle of Walla Walla spoke to state legislative leaders from around the country in 2013, several wondered aloud afterward, "How can I hire him?" Like other presidents who stay long enough to create dramatic change, VanAusdle has no interest in leaving. But the temptation to lead a much larger college—and enjoy the higher salary and greater visibility that comes with it—might draw other successful leaders away from community colleges just when needed reforms are beginning to take hold.

While the president is essential, change cannot begin and end with his or her efforts and vision. Effective presidents hire others who share their goal of dramatically improving student outcomes and empower those individuals to act. They genuinely listen to ideas and concerns, enjoying the dialogue, learning along the way. They appeal to the reason so many people choose to work at community colleges: because they want to help students who might otherwise have no opportunity to enter the middle class. They make sure that strategic plans and major reform initiatives are developed collaboratively and transparently. They identify those within the institution who want to improve, especially among the faculty, and then encourage them to lead and innovate and celebrate their successes. But none of that will create change unless faculty and staff understand why it is so important to act urgently: too many students are failing.

SHIFTING THE FOCUS TO WHAT MATTERS MOST

Colleges have long been funded based on how many students enroll, not on how well students perform. For decades, that's how deans, department chairs, and other leaders have measured themselves. An institution is successful if it fills more seats; a department is successful if it gets more students to take its courses. This was no different at Valencia College, where numbers contained in the eagerly pored-over annual enrollment report (called the "instructional productivity report," though it didn't have anything to do with the productivity of students or the college) were the coin of the realm. When Sandy Shugart became Valencia's president, he realized that faculty and staff would never be able to improve results for students as long as they used the students' mere presence as the primary yardstick.

"As long as they had these reports, getting them to focus on student outcomes would be an uphill battle," Shugart says. So the enrollment reports were replaced by ones that focused on student outcomes. Did students complete and pass their courses? Did they enroll in the next courses? Did they graduate, and do well after graduating?

A change like this may sound simple and obvious, but it happens too rarely. As many college leaders seek to orient their campuses to meet new student success goals—to measure graduation rather than enrollment—they simply layer a new set of metrics on top of an old one. Reports on completion, in courses and programs, are delivered alongside enrollment reports. But if leaders are to shift thinking, it is just as important for them to eliminate one focus as it is to add another. If departments still get their funding based on enrollment and that is what long-standing reports emphasize, it is much harder for leaders and staff to focus on new goals around student success.

Another, even bigger challenge for a president who believes that student outcomes are in dire need of improvement is to get a critical mass of colleagues to believe that too. Colleges are traditionally conservative institutions, resistant to change even when current practice yields poor results.[8] Improvements tend to be incremental: supports are built around existing program structures; new programs are tested in small pilots but rarely taken to scale; facilities are reconfigured or expanded to meet the ever-growing demand. Exceptional presidents know very well that making change at a slow pace isn't sufficient anymore.

They also know when to stop doing what doesn't work, as quickly as possible. Not every great idea succeeds at first (or at all). When Valencia tries a new approach, or continues an old one, Shugart always asks his staff, "Is it working? How do you know?" Good leaders never assume that practitioners will be as committed to an approach as their cabinet is. They know that what looks good on paper may not work in reality. So they make sure that reforms are introduced with benchmarks to measure them by. West Kentucky's move to a computer-delivered model of developmental education didn't show strong results at first, so the college went back at it. Like other successful leaders, Veazey had created a culture where people were not afraid to admit failure. No matter how hard it is to end a failing practice, good leaders ensure that it happens whenever the results show it's necessary.

PLANNING FOR BIG CHANGE

When Valencia reoriented its focus from enrollment to student success, the college had to change much more than its reports. Significant reforms were introduced in the tenure process, student counseling and guidance, registration procedures, and more. It is quite clear that moving an institution to significantly greater student outcomes requires some measure of disruption—and a great leader who can pull it off.

One tool commonly used to create disruption is also one of the most time-honored: the strategic plan. Strategic plans are often the place where big ideas go to die. Numerous committees at the college gather and recite their departments' or divisions' typical requests: new faculty, more space, new programs. Even when nothing is wrong with these practices, they rarely add up to a strategic plan that is likely to improve student success college-wide.

Effective presidents avoid that pitfall. They use the strategic plan to make sure that all of the college's work flows from the clear and powerful goal of improved student outcomes, detailed in a document that everyone understands and that reflects broad buy-in. It's the ultimate clarifier in a complicated landscape.

Leaders can rarely (if ever) achieve enduring, effective change if they simply mandate reforms from above. Most community colleges are complicated institutions with dozens of programs and thousands of students. At institutions of any size, departments are often deeply independent, with long histories of making decisions unencumbered by administrators, defended by notions of academic freedom. One of the most important qualities of great community college presidents, then, is the ability to build a culture of urgency throughout their institutions, so that administrators, faculty, and staff can be partners in reform. The strategic planning process is a great place to begin that work.

Effective colleges start with an exploration of detailed student success data revealing common college-wide challenges: maybe that 12 percent of students who enter underprepared ever get degrees, or that African American students complete at half the rate of white students, or that students who graduate from certain programs earn less than $10 per hour. With a clear, shared understanding of what needs to be fixed, committees are charged with creating big ideas to change outcomes on a large scale. For instance, given how infrequently remedial students ever made it to credit-bearing classes (let alone a degree) at Miami Dade College and Broward College, it was not enough for faculty and staff to tutor some students in the same old developmental courses. Rather, plans were drawn up to fundamentally change the way remediation is taught to every student. Low graduation rates for all kinds of students at Brazosport College made clear that creating student success classes only for students who start behind was inadequate—instead, these classes were required for everyone.

Similar data at Kingsborough College led to the establishment of learning communities—not just for a few entering students but for two-fifths of all freshmen.

Strategic plans at Valencia are built around what the school calls "big ideas," or, as Shugart puts it, "fulcrums for change . . . rallying points for action." Informed by data, these ideas emerge through a process of input that extends beyond committee meetings (which Shugart believes "often accomplish nothing except defending the status quo") to surveys and even technology-assisted "high-bandwidth meetings." At these meetings, large numbers of stakeholders are broken into groups for facilitated conversations, with the goal of quick and informed consensus on college priorities—a process that can take months, if not years, when handled by traditional committees. These new ways of making decisions are in and of themselves forms of change, breaking habits that have led to the same old results.

In the end, the ideas that have emerged are conceptual but clear: students must get a good start in their very first college classes if they are to finish; students need an early and persistent connection to a degree pathway if they are to sustain commitment; learning assessment is critical not as an accountability tool, but as a means for professors to become better teachers. With these shared ideas in mind, community colleges can more easily implement strategies, tactics, and even step-by-step action plans that will yield dramatic changes in registration processes, tools to guide students to completion, tenure processes, and professional development.

Exceptional presidents collaborate but remain in charge of strategic planning, running it out of their offices and remaining at the center of the work. "If the president doesn't lend her gravity to this process, it's generally going to be considered a pro forma plan," Shugart says.

ALLOCATING RESOURCES FOR STUDENT SUCCESS

Community colleges have scarce resources but serve many functions, including work force training, preparation for the final two years of a bachelor's degree, developmental education, and noncredit education ranging from English language to ceramics. Accordingly, the allocation of resources often appears irrational. Nursing programs almost always have long waiting lists and successful graduates, while other programs are underenrolled, fail to lead to good jobs, or both. Colleges struggle to fund adequate support services or financial aid for students at risk of dropping out, while merit scholarship programs are given to well-off students who are quite likely to succeed without financial assistance. And athletic facilities used by relatively few students are maintained even when classrooms and tutoring centers are overcrowded.

Especially in the decentralized decision-making context that characterizes community (and other) colleges—where faculty and staff committees decide on new programs, curriculum design, assessment strategies, and more—reallocating resources can be exceptionally difficult. But the best community college presidents lead institutions that manage to do it nonetheless, that remove funds where they don't fuel improvement and increase them where they do. To these presidents, serving as an effective steward of the budget means not just overseeing proper fiscal management but also ensuring that resources are consistently allocated in ways that align with the student success mission.

This can lead to unpopular decisions. Closing anything on a community college campus is risky; controversy is inevitable. Every program has faculty and staff who rely on it for their livelihood and who see the value it brings to students. These constituents, and their colleagues, vote on various committees and can often stop the closure of a program or prevent funding cuts. Effective leaders have established the urgency for improving student outcomes, which gives them a measure of political cover; they can often bring a critical mass of people on board through effective communication. Notably, they are willing to take risks and upset people.

So while sports are often sacrosanct at colleges, that didn't stop Sandy Shugart from convincing his colleagues at Valencia, after a yearlong conversation, that the big gymnasium would serve students better as tutoring and advising space than as a facility for the small number of students who play intramurals. Eduardo Padron, the president of Miami Dade College, reduced the number of sports teams from thirty-five to five. "This change was very difficult," he recalls. "We underestimated the power of coaches to support their programs and protest their elimination." Padron, like other strong presidents, prevailed by listening to everyone's concerns and "humanizing the process," he says. In the end, with support from his board, he held on to his convictions while maintaining relationships, so that he would survive to make the next set of brave decisions needed to improve student outcomes.

When leaders are singularly focused on student success, data serve as a powerful tool to set goals for improvement and determine whether they are being met. In such a climate, program closure is not about personalities and preferences; the data both drive where money is allocated and help leaders press their case. VanAusdle at Walla Walla is constantly analyzing which programs are graduating students into well-paying jobs and which are not; everyone on campus knows that the facts, rather than passions, drive decisions about what to close and what to expand.

There are many popular strategies that have worked at some community colleges and are broadly accepted as possible ways to help students succeed.[9] But sometimes they don't work at a certain school. Good leaders understand that what matters most is what actually moves students forward on their campuses. For instance, while learning communities are effective in some schools, they weren't at Northern Virginia Community College. So, despite the initial investment, NOVA disassembled its learning communities when they were found to have no impact on student success. At other institutions, the strategy might have been continued, tweaked here or there until it demonstrated marginal improvement that justified the honest efforts of staff and faculty. But that doesn't mean it would ever have become cost-effective when compared to other programs that could use the same amount of resources. Absent focused leadership, decentralized decision making can lead to acceptance of every initiative as equally worthy, and rob truly effective efforts of the resources they need. Unless some interventions are stopped, the best ones cannot receive the resources they need to succeed at scale.

Community colleges can't expect to squeeze water from a stone, be it a cash-strapped family or a cash-strapped government. So good leaders have to think creatively to save money. "The new normal requires us to challenge ourselves on the cost equation," says NOVA's Robert Templin. Some approaches that the college believes to be good educationally are also smart fiscally: using technology to deliver some remedial instruction so student-teacher ratios can increase; allowing students seeking certain certificates to receive credit for demonstrating competencies they learned elsewhere; outsourcing some job training to community nonprofits already experienced in that work. As well, NOVA has identified places where it can earn money and do what it does well, such as offering safety courses for employees of the airline industry and developing expertise in educating international students, who pay more than twice what state residents do.

Above all, at effective colleges, leaders do not use lack of funding as an excuse. The things that matter most get the most. Valencia College receives among the smallest per-pupil contributions of any community college in one of the region's lowest-funded states. While Sandy Shugart would like for his college to be funded comparably to other schools, he and his colleagues have chosen an "abundance mentality." "We have less money than anybody, but we don't talk about that," he says. "Our assumption is, there is more than enough money to do the things we really care about." In part, that's because the college has stopped spending money on many things that don't work.

UNDERSTANDING THAT THE COLLEGE IS NOT A DESTINATION

A multitude of institutional decisions impact students from the time they enroll in a community college to the time they graduate. But if leaders consider only what happens to students on their watches, they misunderstand the role of the college and miss out on crucial opportunities for innovation. "Follow the students," Templin says. "Where are they coming from and where they are going will tell you where to develop partnerships to help students."

Community colleges are not a destination, even though many people say with pride that they are. They are a bridge, from and to other destinations. "Our students are not experiencing us just as single institutions, but as ecosystems or networks of higher education institutions," Shugart said recently in a speech to an accrediting board. "They swirl in and among, stop out, start back, change majors, change departments, change colleges. And because this was exceptional fifty years ago, when we were in college, we continue to think it is the exception. It is now the norm and likely to remain so."[10]

This means that leaders need to think differently. Presidents whose community colleges have good student outcomes pay a lot of attention to how they can help K–12 students get ready for college. They pay attention to the universities students transfer to and the employers who hire them. Those partnerships pay off in big ways, by ensuring that students are prepared for community college, and whatever comes next.

The University of Central Florida is a popular destination for Valencia students: most students who get associate of arts degrees at Valencia transfer within three years to UCF. A decade ago, the university, one of the nation's largest, was in danger of becoming harder to access. Admissions were growing more selective, and the school, traditionally a commuter college, built thousands of dorm rooms and was starting to accept more students from outside the area to fill them. Shugart and other local community colleges worked with UCF to develop a program that guarantees admission to students who received an associate's degree at their schools. But that's not all: staff from UCF and Valencia collaborated to advise students, align curriculum, and track student success. Shugart knows that it doesn't matter how well students do at Valencia if they aren't succeeding at UCF.

Understanding the college's role as a bridge to employment is crucial too. Successful presidents like VanAusdle and Deb Shepard at Lake Area Technical Institute are in weekly contact with local business and economic development leaders to understand what jobs are and will be available to students, what skills they'll need, and how the college can support and even drive local development so graduates have opportunities. That kind of communication leads colleges to add degree programs in high-needs fields, such as alternative energy, advanced machining, and computer security.

College presidents also have to act as a bridge to K–12 education, especially given the large numbers of students who arrive at community college underprepared and the difficulty of delivering effective remedial instruction. The president of Santa Barbara City College meets twice a month with the local school superintendent, and deans meet regularly with high school principals. Among the fruits of this collaboration is a mandatory curriculum the school system and college developed together to orient high school students to college and get them thinking about careers. David Cash, superintendent of the Santa Barbara Unified School District, attributed improvements in his graduates' college readiness in large part to the willingness of the college leaders to innovate in partnership. "I've been a superintendent in three other communities with city colleges, and there's nothing like the relationship here," he says.

Bridges can also be built across multiple expanses. At Northern Virginia Community College, leaders realized that low-income

Hispanic high schoolers, unlike their wealthier peers, were not starting, much less graduating, college. Conversations with community organizations and K–12 administrators revealed multiple reasons: too few thought college was accessible or affordable, many were underprepared when they finished high school, and those that started college got sidetracked as they tried to balance the relentless demands of work with a not-so-clear path to a degree. Rather than take on just one challenge, the college tackled them all through the new Pathway to the Baccalaureate program. Beginning in tenth grade, low-income students receive college counseling and academic remediation, and they are offered a deal: if they complete the required courses, they are guaranteed a place not just at NOVA, but at George Mason University for their junior and senior years.

Today, seven thousand five hundred students are in the Pathway pipeline, two-thirds of them minority students and most from families with low enough income to receive Pell Grants. While the program has not been in place long enough for Pathway students to complete their bachelor's degrees, they are wildly successful by every other measure: 86 percent enter college, 98 percent earn college credit in their first year (rather than taking just noncredit remedial courses), and nearly twice as many attain associate's degrees compared to other NOVA students.

CHOOSING AND DEVELOPING LEADERS

The people best suited to lead community colleges to higher levels of student success in the twenty-first century are willing to take risks, yet trustees tasked with hiring presidents often favor the risk-averse. Trustees put a lot of weight in a candidate's likability and charisma as a public speaker and relationship builder. While it is important to be liked, it is more important to have proven that you can get others to buy in to your vision and motivate and empower them to act. Trustees often look at a prospective president's history of fiscal management but not that person's proven ability to lead community colleges (or other institutions) to much better outcomes. And trustees often assume that community colleges should be led by people who have come through academia, when in truth the attributes of great presidents align as well (or better) to what candidates may have proven in business, or nonprofit organizations, or other complex organizations that demand leaders who are strategic change managers, willing to take smart risks, and capable of following those risks through to results.

This isn't to say that people who came through the college ranks can't make great community college leaders. Every one of the Aspen Prize finalist colleges are led by presidents who arrived in their current positions with substantial prior college experience. Considering the (often neglected) importance of focusing on teaching and learning, there are undeniable benefits from having a firsthand understanding of the classroom. And given that professors play a considerable role in community college governance, if presidents don't understand how to speak to and work with faculty, it is highly unlikely that they will be able to create the kind of change needed to improve student success. But the training one receives for a life in academia and the traits and habits one acquires as a teacher aren't necessarily the ones that enable a leader to catalyze and oversee major organizational change.

This divergence was highlighted in a 2009 paper written by Charles Blaich and Kathy Wise.[11] As director and associate director, respectively, of the Center of Inquiry in the Liberal Arts at Wabash College in Indiana, Blaich and Wise led two consortia of colleges committed to increasing the use of learning assessments to improve student outcomes. After five years, they concluded that only three of twenty-two institutions introduced changes based on assessment data they gathered in the project and assessed the impact of those changes.

One of the central reasons the other nineteen schools did not reach their standard, according to Blaich and Wise, is because in academia, collecting and evaluating information is far more important than acting on it. "Scholarship is built around the process of gathering and reflecting on evidence and information for the sake of gathering and reflecting on more evidence," they wrote. In the liberal arts especially, scholarly research "eschews application. Its success is based on the fact that it generates more questions . . . not on whether it creates practical changes outside the world of scholarship."

Especially given the current context—increased accountability for results, intense competition for students, the potential to completely change the way instruction is delivered due to technological advances—it is critical that leaders act on the information they have rather than waiting until better information is available. With under 40 percent of students graduating or transferring to a four-year institution, today's community college students cannot wait for tomorrow's answers. So their leaders cannot act with the restrained deliberation learned from decades in academia.

If we are to recruit and retain leaders who are willing to act now, with the information they have, we need to take both a broader and more refined view of who might make a good community college president. Future leaders have to deliver degrees more efficiently. They will likely need to reinvent entire systems. Especially at the lowest performing community colleges, where graduation rates are in the single digits, presidents must commit deeply to educating the students traditionally served by community colleges and focus intensely on building a culture that can consistently drive toward measurable improvements in effectiveness and efficiency—something corporate boards seek when hiring leaders to restructure underperforming companies. In large, urban K–12 school districts, where superintendents nearly always worked as teachers, then principals, then district administrators, the doors have opened over the last two decades to a host of nontraditional leaders: attorneys, city managers, corporate CEOs.

No matter where leaders come from, they need to be trained to meet the challenges they'll face. Many of the nontraditional K–12 leaders in big cities (as well as many from typical backgrounds) have completed a training program created by the foundation of billionaire Eli Broad. The program is built around the understanding that the kind of disruptive innovation urban school districts desperately need is quite different from how education leaders typically approach improvement: slowly and incrementally, if at all, with an unhealthy attachment to the status quo.

Community college training programs need a similar refocus. For starters, future leaders should be trained to align all of their efforts—instructional, fiscal, and otherwise—with the goal of improving student outcomes. They should learn how to use data to identify the most important problems and measure whether solutions are working. They should be taught that building relationships to inspire change inside the college is just as important as building relationships outside of it.

There's wide agreement that community colleges cannot be great without great presidents. What people have been slower to understand is that what defines a great president has changed. Today's students, and tomorrow's, need leaders who will take risks on their behalf, and put their success squarely at the heart of every decision.

Conclusion

THE PATH AHEAD

Urgency and Uncertainty

COMMUNITY COLLEGES HAVE ALWAYS BEEN appreciated and recognized by their own communities. Now, though, they are under brighter lights, enjoying a far more intense and broad measure of attention. Constrained family budgets and mounting student debt—which recently surpassed $1 trillion nationally—have led more students to consider community college as an affordable path straight to a job or on-ramp to a bachelor's degree. The federal government, too, is increasingly pinning its hopes on community colleges, as America's global preeminence in higher education continues to wane.

Community colleges are responding with renewed urgency and focus. Longtime community college advocates are calling for better student outcomes, using language typically reserved for critics: access is not enough; completion rates are unacceptable; redesign must be dramatic. Once routinely overlooked, the lowest performing students—those who enter college already behind—now stand at the center of focused efforts to rethink conventional curricular models to improve student success. Increasing numbers of foundations and nonprofit organizations are emerging to support this work through technical assistance, research and evaluation, and venues for professionals to work with and learn from colleagues across the nation.

These are promising developments, but the path ahead is uncertain. Many colleges continue to devise interventions in the decentralized ways they've always done, tweaking existing models. The result: diffuse efforts that take years to develop, pilot, scale, and evaluate and often result in (at best) modest improvements for a small number of students, neither efficient nor extensive enough to please policy makers, let alone serve the majority of students. These reforms too infrequently align with the real lives of students, who wind up dropping out or choosing for-profit competitors.

Many community college leaders, buried by the real challenges their institutions face, acknowledge the changing environment but argue that expectations are already too high and resources too few. These leaders call for incremental reforms. They say they can't *really* be held accountable for achieving dramatically better outcomes, given the deep challenges that their students face in academics and in life.

But students aren't going to become better prepared or have simpler lives anytime soon. Governments are unlikely to increase funding to community colleges; given that, many of today's reforms—even the ones that seem to be helping—are too expensive to scale. If community colleges are to give life to their fundamental and decades-long promise—that they are the gateway to the middle class for disadvantaged Americans—they have to look long and hard for solutions that actually work for the students and with the resources they have now.

The good news, as this book shows, is that several community colleges across the country are finding those solutions. We don't yet fully know how many are transferrable or sustainable. But we do know how the community colleges implementing them—and improving outcomes for their students—define their success. They look at whether students achieve what they most want and need from a higher education: deep, relevant learning, signified by a degree or certificate with proven value in the next stage of their lives (and beyond). Whether students are looking to acquire skills needed for a specific occupation or the critical thinking needed to shift from job to job over a lifetime, they have a right to expect that colleges will do what they can to prepare them for success, measured not just by what they accomplish while on campus, but by how well they do after they graduate.

Exceptional community colleges do not limit themselves to interventions aimed at a single outcome, be that access, learning, equity, completion, or post-graduation success. Strong leaders may, for limited periods of time, pursue just one of those goals as a way to move their institutions beyond the traditional aim of getting students in the door. But they understand that, ultimately, that is not enough.

So these colleges move to award more degrees and certificates while studying whether those credentials actually result in good jobs. They work to improve teaching so that students learn measurably more, while analyzing data and engaging deeply with employers and four-year colleges to ensure that learning aligns with what students will need to be successful after they graduate. They make sure initiatives to increase the number and rates of students who graduate don't inadvertently curtail access for minority students or widen achievement gaps.

To achieve these goals, exceptional community colleges frequently adopt proven practices from other institutions and avoid significant mistakes they learn from other college leaders brave enough to disclose them. If more of the nation's twelve hundred institutions are to improve, they cannot all invent solutions to every problem; there simply isn't time for that. So it is important that promising practices continue to be developed, their impacts researched, and, where they are truly effective and efficient at scale, that they be replicated on other campuses.

At the same time, exceptional community colleges also demonstrate that culture drives successful practice, not the other way around. And while cultures cannot be expected to go from dysfunctional to high performing overnight, evidence shows that through intentional effort, colleges can develop broad and deep support for exceptional outcomes. In high performing community colleges, change begins with shared urgency and specific plans for student success driven by clear data, informed by thoughtful conversations, implemented with tenacity and flexibility, and then regularly evaluated and adjusted. Always, the driving question is, "Are we enabling a significantly larger number of students to succeed at higher levels?" Leaders resolutely align resources and incentives with this goal, even if that means closing long-standing programs, changing tenure systems, or spending a portion of constrained budgets off-campus if that is what it takes to help more students succeed.

These complex, culture-changing, and often risky efforts are the kinds of practices that have enabled the exceptional institutions profiled in this book to achieve high and continually improving graduation and transfer rates, to shrink or even eliminate gaps in completion between minority and white students, and to routinely place graduates in jobs that pay good salaries and in four-year colleges where they are likely to receive a bachelor's degree.

Without exception, these high performing cultures were built by and around people. Trustees hired presidents capable of complex change management and committed to taking risks. Faculty committed to becoming better instructors so that students could learn more. Staff throughout the college came to understand and deeply believe that students deserve every chance to succeed, even if that means making radical changes in daily practices and routines to better accommodate students' needs.

Only within such high performing cultures will community colleges be able to resolve the enduring and emerging challenges they face: how to help students, who so often enter far behind, learn well, graduate in a reasonable amount of time, and earn a valuable credential; how to ensure that faculty, including an ever-growing number of adjunct professors, become better instructors and contribute more to students' success; how to employ technology and reenvision faculty roles to create greater efficiencies without compromising instructional quality.

None of these challenges will be met easily. The states, systems, and communities that understand how important these institutions are to the U.S. economy and to the democratic ideal of equal opportunity must challenge the entire sector to do better. But they must also recognize and support community colleges that have already made and continue to make great improvements, and they must help others achieve those successes too.

It is imperative that more community colleges, led by highly capable leaders, transform how they approach these challenges. The decades-long investment made by our nation—and so many talented and committed individuals—in community colleges has fueled unparalleled educational opportunity. In many countries, children are locked at an early age into a stratified education system that determines the kinds of jobs and wages they'll have access to for the rest of their lives. In the United States, though, nearly two-thirds of adults attend or have attended college. We have committed as a society to the idea that the full range of educational opportunities should be open to all, regardless of class, race, ethnicity, or age. Community colleges have been and will continue to be the fulcrum of that commitment.

Community colleges can build on this accomplishment, but they must act quickly to ensure that the promise they extend is fulfilled—not only in access, but in success, and not only for traditional students, but for all the diverse individuals who walk through their doors. This book is both a celebration of those colleges that are leading the way and a call to action for policy makers, leaders, researchers, trustees, and communities to support other colleges in following suit. There is a great potential waiting to be unlocked—in the nation's community colleges as institutions, and in each student who enrolls in one hoping and expecting to succeed.

APPENDIX A

Seven Colleges Featured in This Book

O F THE COLLEGES PROFILED IN THIS BOOK, seven frequently highlighted were winners of and finalists with distinction for the Aspen Prize for Community College Excellence. Serving very different student populations with different mixes of programs in dramatically different communities, these colleges have one thing in common: they achieve exceptional and rapidly improving levels of student success.

Kingsborough Community College
Brooklyn, New York (urban)
Finalist with Distinction, 2013

Enrollment: 25,000

Description: Kingsborough is an urban community college offering a range of programs, largely focused on transfer-directed associate's degrees. About 80 percent of students are traditional college-age, 40 percent attend part-time, about half are minorities, and 61 percent receive Pell Grants.

Exceptional outcomes: Kingsborough graduation and transfer rates are above the national average for all community colleges, and far above the average for large urban institutions. The majority of students who enter Kingsborough transfer to a four-year college, and labor market outcomes are strong: five years after completing their two-year degree, Kingsborough graduates earn, on average, $41,000 per year, higher than the average for other workers in the region.

Distinctive attributes: Kingsborough is best known for its fifty learning communities, which connect groups of students in multiple linked courses, include strong professional development for professors, and require students to participate in regular advising. A recent study demonstrated that Kingsborough's learning communities notably improve student success, with increases in retention rates more than offsetting the cost. Kingsborough has also implemented developmental education programs with unusually high success rates and the first national Single Stop program, which connects low-income students with social and financial services.

Lake Area Technical Institute
Watertown, South Dakota (small town/rural)
Finalist with Distinction, 2011 and 2013

Enrollment: 1,700

Description: Lake Area Technical Institute (LATI) is a technical college that offers thirty work force training programs. Over 80 percent of students are traditional college-age and attend full-time, almost all are white, and 41 percent receive Pell Grants.

Exceptional outcomes: At 76 percent, the college's three-year graduation rate is among the highest in the nation. Wage outcomes for graduates are consistently higher than for other workers in the region.

Distinctive attributes: As with some other technical colleges (but very few general education programs), programs at LATI are designed so students have clear schedules, make few if any course choices, and attend full-time with a set schedule. Given the high percentage of students on need-based aid, it is notable that LATI has virtually eliminated the necessity for remedial education by establishing a different set of readiness requirements for entry into each of its programs of study.

Miami Dade College
Miami, Florida (urban)
Finalist with Distinction, 2011

Enrollment: 100,000

Description: The largest public college in the nation, Miami Dade College is a multicampus comprehensive community college in south Florida. While it offers a range of career and technical programs, the majority of credentials it confers are transfer-oriented. About two-thirds of students are traditional college-age; almost 90 percent are minorities, mostly Hispanic (70 percent); and about a third receive Pell Grants.

Exceptional outcomes: Miami Dade has rapidly increased graduation and transfer rates, which are above the national average for all community colleges and far above the average for large urban institutions. In a region with more than 12 percent unemployment, recent graduates have exceptionally strong labor market outcomes, earning an average of $63,000 per year five years after completing their degrees.

Distinctive attributes: Long recognized as a leader in its community, Miami Dade has educated major leaders in virtually every aspect of civic and economic life. Building on exceptional programs ranging from student academic services to financial aid, Miami Dade is one of a few colleges working with a national program, Completion by Design, to dramatically clarify degree pathways in general education programs.

Santa Barbara City College
Santa Barbara, California (urban)
Co-winner, 2013

Enrollment: 29,000

Description: Santa Barbara City College (SBCC) offers a range of programs, most focused on transfer-directed associate's degrees. About two-thirds of students are traditional college-age, about two-thirds attend part-time, and a third are minorities (mostly Hispanic).

Exceptional outcomes: Almost two-thirds of SBCC's full-time students graduate or transfer within three years, a rate far above the national average and particularly impressive for a large, highly diverse college. Hispanic and African American students also graduate and transfer at a rate well above the national average for those groups (48 percent, compared to 30 percent). About half of students who enter SBCC transfer to a four-year college, and just over half complete their four-year degrees within six years of having entered the community college.

Distinctive attributes: SBCC provides a wide range of resources—and sets high expectations—for all students, with a focus on the large and growing number of Hispanic students. Strong student success rates have been tied to accelerated developmental education programs, a writing center staffed by trained professionals, and peer tutors working in many courses. SBCC also maintains an unusually strong set of programs with local high schools, working with students from eighth grade through high school graduation to ensure that they are academically, socially, and financially prepared for college.

Valencia College
Orlando, Florida (urban)
Winner, 2011

Enrollment: 50,000

Description: Valencia College is a comprehensive, multicampus community college in central Florida that offers a comprehensive range of programs, including transfer-directed associate's degrees, career technical certificates, and continuing professional education. The majority of credentials Valencia awards are transfer-oriented. Most students are traditional college-age, about half are Hispanic or African American, and just over 40 percent receive Pell Grants.

Exceptional outcomes: More than half of Valencia's full-time students graduate or transfer within three years, a rate well above the national average and particularly impressive for a large, highly diverse college. Hispanic and African American students also graduate and transfer at rates well above the national averages for those groups. Over the five years prior to the school's winning the Aspen Prize, enrollment increased 40 percent and credentials awarded increased even more: 96 percent for associate of arts degrees, 60 percent for associate of science degrees, and 59 percent for other credentials.

Distinctive attributes: Valencia has one of the nation's most successful transfer programs, built on guaranteed admission to the selective University of Central Florida, and strong technical programs, each with embedded career advisers. The college has a unique faculty development and tenure process, designed to ensure that professors work to improve their teaching and communicate with one another along the way. Other interventions aim at creating incentives for students to use services, clarifying pathways, and limiting the kinds of student choices that result in poor completion rates.

Walla Walla Community College
Co-winner, 2013; Finalist with Distinction, 2011
Walla Walla, Washington (small town/rural)

Enrollment: 8,600

Description: Walla Walla Community College is a comprehensive community college, offering programs in both career technical and general education/transfer, but it is best known for its exceptional work force development programs, including wind energy, nursing, agricultural machine technology, and winemaking. About half of students are traditional college-age, half attend part-time, 20 percent are minorities (most of them Hispanic), and 43 percent receive Pell Grants.

Exceptional outcomes: Over half of Walla Walla's full-time students graduate or transfer within three years, a rate well above the national average. Despite a majority of students entering below college-ready standards, 45 percent of students transfer to four-year colleges. Even more impressive are wage outcomes for graduates. Recent graduates earn, on average, $42,000 per year and, five years after graduating, they average $57,000, which is dramatically higher than for other workers in the region.

Distinctive attributes: Strong work force programs lie at the heart of Walla Walla's success. By analyzing labor market data and working closely with others on regional economic development, the community college has not only aligned its programs with what is needed in the regional economy, but also has helped envision a new economy and trained students with the skills needed to drive economic growth. Walla Walla provides strong advising to students, bolstered substantially by exceptional technology-based systems. The college has also developed uniquely effective partnerships—with a Native American tribe to restore the local watershed through a water management center, and with the state corrections department to educate prisoners.

West Kentucky Community and Technical College
Finalist with Distinction, 2011
Paducah, Kentucky (small town/rural)

Enrollment: 10,900

Description: West Kentucky Community and Technical College (WKCTC) is a comprehensive community college, with about two-thirds of its credentials in work force development programs. About half of students are traditional college-age, 65 percent attend part-time, 9 percent are minorities, and half receive Pell Grants.

Exceptional outcomes: Just under half of WKCTC's full-time students graduate or transfer within three years, a rate well above the national average. Of the students who transfer, about half complete their four-year degrees within six years of having entered the community college, a very high rate given the large part-time population. In fact, WKCTC transfers perform better than other Kentucky students in their junior and senior years at area four-year colleges.

Distinctive attributes: WKCTC's strong culture is built on using course and campus-wide student learning assessments to determine areas for improvement and then acting on that information. WKCTC is a central contributor to the local economy, training most of the nurses and other allied health workers for the region's substantial health care sector. Based on very strong ties to regional economic development players, the college readily understands and effectively responds to the needs of local industries and workers, having created new programs for the chemical industry and riverboat operators and having expanded existing programs quickly to help train displaced workers.

APPENDIX B

Aspen Prize Data

To assess the four elements of excellence—learning, completion, labor market, and equitable outcomes—the Aspen Institute accesses multiple sources to collect quantitative data and qualitative information about the finalist colleges.

QUANTITATIVE DATA

The Integrated Postsecondary Education Data System (IPEDS)

- Credentials awarded per one hundred FTE (encompassing both full-time and part-time students)
  - For all students
  - For underrepresented minority (URM) students
- Three-year graduation/transfer rate
  - For all students
  - For underrepresented minority students
- Retention rate (first-to-second year)
- Data on five years of improvement on three measures: retention rate, three-year graduation/transfer rate, credentials awarded per one hundred FTE
- Achievement gap between white and URM students

National Student Clearinghouse

- Four-year transfer rate
- Bachelor's degree completion rate

Institutional Data
- Institutional data on work force outcomes based on surveys
- Six-year cohort analysis on completion and transfer outcomes

State Unemployment Insurance Records Matched with Institutional Cohort Data
- Class of 2006 employment information
  —Job placement rate one year and five years after graduation
  —Rate of continuous employment
  —Annualized salaries and wages five years after graduation
- Class of 2011 employment information
  —Job placement rate at graduation and one year after graduation
  —Rate of continuous employment
  —Annualized salaries and wages one year after graduation

QUALITATIVE INFORMATION

- Assessment of Peter Ewell and Karen Paulson (National Center for Higher Education Management Systems) regarding how the institution collects and uses information about student learning to improve learning outcomes
- Assessment of expert site visitors based on information collected before and during site visits including (1) meetings with institutional leaders, professors, department chairs, deans, staff, students, and employers, and (2) documents submitted by each institution, including strategic plans, accreditation reports, and program review reports

CONTEXTUAL INFORMATION

Because community colleges work with many different student populations in communities with varying challenges, Aspen collects a significant amount of contextual data to share with the Finalist Selection Committee and Prize Jury.

The Integrated Postsecondary Education Data System (IPEDS)

- Percentage of students attending part-time
- Percentage of vocational/technical awards (out of all awards conferred)
- Percentage of nontraditional-age students (twenty-five and older)
- Percentage of underrepresented minority students (disaggregated by African American, Hispanic, and Native American students)
- Percentage of Pell Grant recipients

U.S. Census

- Median family income of service area
- Urbanicity
- Percentage of underrepresented minorities in the service area
- Average annual county new hire wage

U.S. Bureau of Labor Statistics

- County unemployment rate
- County five-year employment change rate
- Average annual county wage

Institutional Data

- Percentage of students entering needing remedial education

NOTES

FOREWORD

1. Projections from the Georgetown University Center on Education and the Workforce, "Recovery: Job Growth and Education Requirements Through 2020," http://cew.georgetown.edu/recovery2020/.

INTRODUCTION

1. American Association of Community Colleges, *Reclaiming the American Dream: A Report from the 21st-Century Commission on the Future of Community Colleges* (Washington, DC: American Association of Community Colleges, 2012).
2. In February 2013, the National Conference of State Legislatures (NCSL) reported that eighteen states had either adopted or were adopting performance funding, based on how many students complete courses and degrees, with an additional twenty-four states in "formal discussions." See the map on the NCSL's Web site at the National Conference of State Legislatures, "Performance Funding for Higher Education," http://www.ncsl.org/issues-research/educ/performance-funding.aspx.
3. For instance, recent reports by the research organization MDRC on learning communities demonstrate that individual strategies are only sometimes effective; and the evaluation of the first five years of Achieving the Dream, an effort to improve completion through data analysis and action, reveals the challenges of institution-wide reform. See Mary G. Visher et al., *The Effects of Learning Communities for Students in Developmental Education: A Synthesis of Findings from Six Community Colleges* (New York: Community College Research Center, Teachers College, Columbia University, 2012); Elizabeth Zachary Rutschow et al., *Turning the Tide: Five Years of Achieving the Dream in Community Colleges* (New York: Community College Research Center, Teachers College, Columbia University, 2012).
4. An analysis of data contained in the Integrated Postsecondary Education Data System (IPEDs) shows graduation rates for first-time, full-time, credential-seeking community college students decreased from 23.6 percent

for the cohort that started in 2000 to 20.4 percent for the cohorts that started in 2006 and 2007. See U.S. Department of Education, National Center for Education Statistics, *2011 Digest of Education Statistics*, Table 345 [Integrated Postsecondary Education Data System (IPEDS), Fall 2001 and Spring 2002 through Spring 2011, Graduation Rates component]. More recent data shows an uptick in overall college graduation rates, but it remains unclear what is causing the increase. See Catherine Rampell, "Data Reveal a Rise in College Degrees Among Americans," *New York Times*, June 12, 2013, http://www.nytimes.com/2013/06/13/education/a-sharp-rise-in-americans-with-college-degrees.html?smid=pl-share.

5. While the majority of this book is based on learning from the first year of the Aspen Prize, it has been supplemented by select findings from the early stages of the second year, the author's research on the community college presidency, and the author's experience at Northern Virginia Community College during a 2008 American Council of Education fellowship.

6. Of the colleges eligible for the Aspen Prize in the first two years, 86 percent applied and met the extensive reporting requirements.

Chapter 1

1. Public Agenda, *With Their Whole Lives Ahead of Them: Myths and Realities About Why So Many Students Fail to Finish College* (San Francisco: Public Agenda, 2011).

2. Thomas Bailey, "Rethinking Developmental Education in Community College," *Community College Research Center Brief*, 2009, no. 40 (Community College Research Center, Teachers College, Columbia University, New York, NY, 2009).

3. Don Hossler et al., *Transfer & Mobility: A National View of Pre-Degree Student Movement in Postsecondary Institutions* (Herndon, VA: National Student Clearinghouse Research Center, 2012).

4. Ibid.

5. African American and Latino students constituted 32.8 percent of public community college enrollment, compared to only 24 percent of enrollment, at all four-year institutions in 2010. See National Center for Education Statistics, "Fall Enrollment in Colleges and Universities" (Washington, DC: Higher Education General Information Series, U.S. Department of Education, 1976 and 1980); National Center for Education Statistics, Integrated Postsecondary Education Data System, "Fall Enrollment Survey," document no. IPEDS-EF:90 (Washington, DC: NCES, 2001–2011).

6. Twenty-two percent of first-time, full-time, degree-seeking students at public two-year colleges had completed a degree or certificate within three years of entry. See Integrated Postsecondary Education Data System, "2011 Graduation Rate Survey," IPEDS document Fall 2008 cohort (Washington, DC: U.S. Department of Education, 2011).

7. See Doug Shapiro et al., *Completing College: A National View of Student Attainment Rates* (Herndon, VA: National Student Clearinghouse Research Center, 2012), 32, which estimates the completion rate of part-time students within six years at less than 20 percent, including students who transferred to other two-year or four-year institutions.

8. Lumina Foundation for Education, a major higher education philanthropy, has as its goal that 60 percent of Americans will hold "high-quality" degrees and credentials by 2025; the Bill & Melinda Gates Foundation aims to help double the number of low-income youth who earn a degree or credential "with value in the workplace" by age twenty-six. See Lumina Foundation, "Lumina Foundation Strategic Plan 2013–2016," http://www.luminafoundation.org/goal_2025.html, and Bill & Melinda Gates Foundation, "New Initiative to Double the Number of Low-Income Students in the U.S. Who Earn a Postsecondary Degree," http://www.gatesfoundation.org/Media-Center/Press-Releases/2008/12/New-Initiative-to-Double-the-Number-of-LowIncome-Students-in-the-US-Who-Earn-a-Postsecondary-Degree. Efforts like the Obama administration's $2 billion, four-year initiative to help community colleges and employers provide job training were created to complement the president's goal to increase postsecondary education attainment. See the White House, "Building American Skills Through Community Colleges," http://www.whitehouse.gov/issues/education/higher-education/building-american-skills-through-community-colleges.

9. The terms *developmental* and *remedial* education are used interchangeably throughout this book to refer to courses that teach reading, writing, and math skills that students are expected to have mastered prior to enrolling in college courses. The preferred term for such courses varies across the country, and no negative connotations are intended by the use of either term.

10. Davis Jenkins and Sung-Woo Cho, "Get with the Program: Accelerating Community College Students' Entry into and Completion of Programs of Study" (working paper, Community College Research Center, Teachers College, Columbia University, New York, NY, 2012) shows that a central predictor of graduation is whether students complete a series of courses

specific to a defined degree program. See also the work of James Rosenbaum at the Institute for Policy Research at Northwestern University.

11. The largest pool of financial aid available to low-income students nationally, Pell Grants, are available to a student for only six years. If a student needs remedial courses before beginning credit classes, this limitation can present a challenge if the student is attending part-time and/or intends to pursue a four-year degree.

12. The majors are business administration, health information technology, human services, information technology, liberal arts and sciences, and urban studies. Even the liberal arts major has a fixed set of courses.

13. In 2012–2013, the New College's first year of operations, 92 percent of students who began in the fall returned in the spring. This compares to an average fall-to-spring retention rate of only 75 percent at community colleges nationally, even when taking into account students who transferred to a different institution. See National Student Clearinghouse Center, "Snapshot Report: Persistence," http://www.studentclearinghouse.info/snapshot/docs/SnapshotReport1-Persistence.pdf.

14. It helps that Florida has strong articulation agreements between the state's two-year and four-year public colleges, and most students who transfer from Miami Dade remain in the state system. No matter their program, there is little difference in what courses students need to take to transfer with junior-year standing.

15. The programs are health sciences, business, biology, criminal justice, and psychology.

16. In 2004–2005, 60 percent of community college students indicated a desire to transfer. See Stephen J. Handel and Ronald A. Williams, *The Promise of the Transfer Pathway: Opportunity and Challenge for Community Colleges Seeking the Baccalaureate Degree* (New York: College Board Advocacy & Policy Center, 2012).

17. The National Student Clearinghouse Research Center report cited in Don Hossler et al., *Transfer & Mobility*, estimates a 20 percent two-year to four-year transfer rate, while the College Board report cited in Handel and Williams, *The Promise of the Transfer Pathway*, estimates a 26 percent national transfer rate.

18. The names of students in this book have been changed.

19. Handel and Williams, *The Promise of the Transfer Pathway*, 24–25.

20. See Phil Oliff, Vincent Palacios, Ingrid Johnson, and Michael Leachman, "Recent Deep State Higher Education Cuts May Harm Students and the

Economy for Years to Come," Center for Budget and Policy Priorities, March 19, 2013, http://www.cbpp.org/cms/?fa=view&id=3927.

21. http://www.whitehouse.gov/the-press-office/2012/02/13/remarks-president-budget.

22. A task force convened by the Century Foundation to consider inequities in U.S. community colleges recommended in 2013 that selective colleges set aside 5 percent of their junior-class seats to students transferring from community colleges. See Century Foundation, *Bridging the Higher Education Divide: Strengthening Community Colleges and Restoring the American Dream* (Washington, DC: Century Foundation Press, 2013). But while a few such colleges have in recent years expanded seats for transfers in recent years as a way to increase diversity, supported by million-dollar grants from the Jack Kent Cooke Foundation, most highly selective colleges have not followed suit.

23. Richard Arum and Josipa Roksa, *Academically Adrift: Limited Learning on College Campuses* (Chicago: University of Chicago Press, 2010).

24. See the National Center on Education and the Economy, "What Does It Really Mean to Be College and Work Ready?: The Mathematics and English Literacy Required of First Year Community College Students," http://www.ncee.org/college-and-work-ready/. The report found that the reading and writing currently required of students in lower-level, credit-bearing community colleges courses is not very complex or cognitively demanding.

25. See Norton W. Grubb, "Getting into the World: Guidance and Counseling in Community Colleges" (working paper, Community College Research Center, Teachers College, Columbia University, New York, NY, 2001); Linda Serra Hagedorn et al., "Transfer Between Community Colleges and Four-Year Colleges: The All American Game," *Community College Journal of Research and Practice* 30, no. 3 (2006).

26. Students have a better chance of graduating when they attend more selective colleges, something low-income students often are not advised to do. See William Bowen, Matthew M. Chingos, and Michael S. McPherson, *Crossing the Finish Line: Completing College at America's Public Universities* (Princeton, NJ: Princeton University Press, 2009); Joshua S. Wyner, John M. Bridgeland, and John J. Diiulio Jr., *Achievement Trap: How America Is Failing Millions of High-Achieving Students from Lower-Income Families* (Washington, DC: Jack Kent Cooke Foundation and Civic Enterprises, 2007); Melissa Roderick et al., *From High School to the Future: Potholes on*

the Road to College (Chicago: University of Chicago Consortium on Chicago School Research, 2008).

27. By comparison, institutional four-year graduation rates can be predicted with a fair degree of certainty by examining two factors: average incoming SAT and ACT scores and the percentage of students receiving Pell Grants. But very few community college programs require the SAT or ACT for entry, and only 37 percent of community college students receive Pell Grants. (U.S. Dept. of Education, 2011 IPEDS Student Financial Aid and Net Price Survey).

28. Bailey, "Rethinking Developmental Education."

29. Analysis of the most recent available IPEDS data on first-time, full-time community college students conducted by the National Center for Higher Education Management Systems for the Aspen Institute, 2013.

30. Conversation with Mark Herzog, former chancellor of the Connecticut Community College System.

31. See National Student Clearinghouse Research Center, "Outcomes of Students Who Transferred from Two-Year to Four-Year Institutions (Four Years After Transfer)," http://www.studentclearinghouse.info/snapshot/docs/SnapshotReport8-GradRates2-4Transfers.pdf.

32. The case for not including two-year to two-year transfer in the definition of student success is made convincingly in Thomas Bailey, Davis Jenkins, and Timothy Leinbach, "Graduation Rates, Student Goals, and Measuring Community College Effectiveness," *Community College Research Center Brief*, 2005, no. 28.

33. A proprietary provider of transfer data, the National Student Clearinghouse, has stepped into this void. Originally set up to track students' loan obligations, the clearinghouse keeps track of over 90 percent of students, even after they transfer. But transfer data it collects about individual institutions can only be accessed by those institutions themselves, or their state systems, if they subscribe to the service (and for a high price). Thus, while community colleges can pay to figure out how many of their students transfer to four-year colleges and obtain bachelor's degrees, they cannot compare their results to peer institutions.

Chapter 2

1. For instance, My Brother's Keeper at Santa Fe College, the Transitional Bilingual Learning Communities at Truman College in Chicago, and MDRC's Opening Doors program in several states.

2. Only 10 percent earn a degree within three years. See Complete College America, *Remediation: Higher Education's Bridge to Nowhere* (Washington, DC: Complete College America, 2012).

3. See Thomas Bailey, "Rethinking Developmental Education in Community College," *Community College Research Center Brief*, 2009, no. 40.

4. William G. Bowen, Matthew M. Chingos, and Michael S. McPherson, *Crossing the Finish Line: Completing College at America's Public Universities* (Princeton, NJ: Princeton University Press, 2009).

5. U.S. Census Bureau, American Community Survey, "Educational Attainment in the United States, 2009: Population Characteristics," http://www .census.gov/prod/2012pubs/p20-566.pdf.

6. William J. Hussar and Tabitha M. Bailey, ed., *Projections of Education Statistics to 2018, 37th Edition*, NCES 2009-062 (Washington, DC: U.S. Department of Education, National Center for Education Statistics, 2009).

7. Given that some states and colleges make remediation optional, the 70 percent does not reflect the percentage of students who *need* remediation—just the share who took it. See the College Board Advocacy & Policy Center's Web tool found at "The Completion Arch: Measuring Community College Student Success," http://completionarch.collegeboard.org/placement/ participation-in-developmental-courses/participation-in-developmental-courses-us.

8. Davis Jenkins, Shanna S. Jaggars, & Josipa Roksa, *Promoting Gatekeeper Course Success Among Community College Students Needing Remediation: Findings and Recommendations from a Virginia Study (Summary Report)* (New York: Community College Research Center, Teachers College, Columbia University, 2009), 10.

9. "While research on best practices in developmental education abounds, little rigorous research exists to demonstrate the effect of these reforms . . . Many of the strategies have not yet been evaluated using more rigorous and reliable research methods, and/or early promising results have not been replicated in other settings." Elizabeth Zachry Rutschow and Emily Schneider, *Unlocking the Gate: What We Know About Improving Developmental Education* (New York: MDRC, 2011), iii.

10. Kay Mills, "Redesigning the Basics: Tennessee's Community Colleges Use Technology to Change Their Approach to Developmental Reading and Math," in *American Higher Education: Journalistic and Policy Perspectives from National CrossTalk*, ed. William H. Trombley and Todd Sallo (San Jose, CA: The National Center for Public Policy and Higher Education, 2012), 99–102.

11. CUNY Start, "Overview and Analysis of Student Outcomes" (unpublished report, City University of New York, 2012).

12. For more on the Virginia reforms, see Kay Mills, *Altered State: How the Virginia Community College System Has Used Achieving the Dream to Improve Student Success* (Boston: Jobs for the Future, 2010).

13. A promising alternative approach being tested in several states, known as the Carnegie Statway, replaces traditional remedial math courses with defined course sequences in statistics or quantitative reasoning. The curriculum, developed by the Carnegie Foundation for the Advancement of Teaching, combines online and in-class instruction and provides intensive student supports. For more information, see Scott Strother, James Van Campen, and Alicia Grunow, *Community College Pathways 2011–2012 Descriptive Report* (Stanford, CA: Carnegie Foundation for the Advancement of Teaching, 2013).

14. "Developmental Math Enrollment" (unpublished report, Office of Institutional Research, Planning and Assessment, Northern Virginia Community College, Springfield, VA, 2013).

15. Basmat Parsad and Laurie Lewis, ed., *Remedial Education at Degree-Granting Postsecondary Institutions in Fall 2000*, NCES 2004-010 (Washington, DC: U.S. Department of Education, National Center for Education Statistics, 2003).

16. See, for example, Clive R. Belfield and Peter M. Crosta, "Predicting Success in College: The Importance of Placement Tests and High School Transcripts" (working paper, Community College Research Center, Teachers College, Columbia University, New York, NY, 2012); Judith Scott-Clayton, "Do High-Stakes Placement Exams Predict College Success?" (working paper, Community College Research Center, Teachers College, Columbia University, New York, NY, 2012).

17. Scott-Clayton, "High-Stakes Placement Exams."

18. In 2007–2008, 40 percent of all undergraduates were twenty-four or older; 60 percent attended part-time or only part of the year; and 25 percent had dependent children. National Center for Education Statistics (NCES), "2012 Digest of Education Statistics" (Washington, DC: Table 242, U.S. Department of Education, 2012); National Center for Education Statistics (NCES), "2007–08 National Postsecondary Student Aid Study" (Washington, DC: NPSAS:08, U.S. Department of Education, 2009).

19. Katherine L. Hughes and Judith Scott-Clayton, "Assessing Developmental Assessment in Community Colleges" (working paper, Community

College Research Center, Teachers College, Columbia University, New York, NY, 2011).

20. Davis Jenkins, Matthew Zeidenberg, and Gregory S. Kienzl, "Educational Outcomes of I-BEST, Washington State Community and Technical College System's Integrated Basic Education and Skills Training Program: Findings from a Multivariate Analysis" (working paper, Community College Research Center, Teachers College, Columbia University, New York, NY, 2009).

21. Among the principles of the joint statement by five organizations: "Enrollment in a gateway college-level course should be the default placement for many more students" and "Additional academic support should be integrated with gateway college-level course content—as a co-requisite, not a pre-requisite." Charles A. Dana Center, *Core Principles for Transforming Remedial Education: A Joint Statement* (Austin: Complete College America, Education Commission of the States, and Jobs for the Future, 2012), 6.

22. Hughes and Scott-Clayton, "Assessing Developmental Assessment."

23. See, for example, Carol A. Tomlinson et al., "Differentiating Instruction in Response to Student Readiness, Interest, and Learning Profile in Academically Diverse Classrooms: A Review of Literature," *Journal for the Education of the Gifted* 27, no. 2/3 (2003): 119–145; Joyce VanTassel-Baska and Tamra Stambaugh, "Challenges and Possibilities for Serving Gifted Learners in the Regular Classroom," *Theory Into Practice*, 44, no. 3 (2005): 211–217.

24. Paul Fain, "Overkill on Remediation?," *Inside Higher Ed*, June 19, 2012, http://www.insidehighered.com/news/2012/06/19/complete-college-america-declares-war-remediation.

25. Thomas Bailey, Katherine L. Hughes, and Shanna Smith, "Law Hamstrings College Remedial Programs," *Hartford Courant*, May 18, 2012, http://articles.courant.com/2012-05-18/news/hc-op-bailey-college-remedial-education-bill-too-r-20120518_1_remedial-classes-community-college-research-center-remedial-education.

26. Complete College America advocates that this solution be adopted as a matter of state policy: "Those who seek to attend a community college with what amounts to little more than a basic understanding of fractions and decimals should be encouraged to enroll in high-quality career certificate programs that embed extra help in the context of each course and lead to jobs that pay well." Complete College America, *Remediation: Higher Education's Bridge to Nowhere* (Washington, DC: Complete College America, 2012), 3.

27. Kati Haycock, "A New Curriculum for All: Aiming High for Other People's Children," *Thinking K–16* 7, no. 1 (2003): 2.
28. Fain, "Overkill on Remediation."
29. Paul Fain, "Behind the Billboards," *Inside Higher Ed*, December 14, 2011, http://www.insidehighered.com/news/2011/12/14/texas-business-groups-billboard-campaign-completion-rates.
30. Alliance for Education, *Saving Now and Saving Later: How High School Reform Can Reduce the Nation's Wasted Remediation Dollars*, (Washington, DC: Alliance for Education, 2011).
31. See Katherine Mangan, "National Group Call for Big Changes in Remedial Education," *Chronicle of Higher Education*, December 13, 2012, http://chronicle.com/article/National-Groups-Call-for-Big/136285/.
32. Heather Hollingsworth, "Experts: Remedial College Classes Need Fixing," *Associated Press*, May 28, 2012, http://news.yahoo.com/experts-remedial-college-classes-fixing-184407870.html.
33. Stan Jones, "Gateway Course Success: Gateway, Not 'Gatekeeper,'" (PowerPoint presentation, Complete College America, Washington, DC, April 2012).
34. For example, university systems that are members of Access to Success—an initiative of the Education Trust in Washington, DC—have pledged by 2015 to cut in half the gaps between the success rates of underrepresented minority students and others. See, for example, Jennifer Engle et al., *Replenishing Opportunity in America: The 2012 Midterm Report of Public Higher Education Systems in the Access to Success Initiative* (Washington, DC: The Education Trust, 2012).
35. One way some community colleges engineer success is by offering merit scholarships (without regard to financial need) to attract better-prepared students, who are often not minorities, which may help completion rates but doesn't serve a goal of equity.

CHAPTER 3

1. Several national organizations are dedicated to improved teaching in higher education, including the National Institute for Learning Outcomes Assessment and the New Leadership Alliance for Student Learning and Accountability. In addition, the Lumina Foundation has sponsored a series of demonstration projects under the banner "Tuning USA," each of which is "a faculty-driven process that identifies what a student should know and be able to do in a chosen discipline when a degree has been earned—an

associate's, bachelor's, or master's." See http://www.luminafoundation.org/ tag/tuning/. However, the focus of these initiatives—improving what students learn and how professors teach—has not received nearly the degree of attention paid to the completion agenda in national and state-level conversations about improving higher education outcomes.

2. See, respectively, the Gates Foundation initiative Completion by Design, the national nonprofit Achieving the Dream, and performance funding policies advocated by Complete College America.

3. Paul Fain, "Facing Facts," *Inside Higher Ed,* May 29, 2012, http://www .insidehighered.com/news/2012/05/29/taking-stock-completion-agendas-benefits-and-limits.

4. Richard Arum and Josipa Roksa, *Academically Adrift: Limited Learning on College Campuses* (Chicago: University of Chicago Press, 2010).

5. The 2011 data is from the National Survey of Student Engagement at Indiana University; the 1961 data is from Philip Babcock and Mindy Marks, "The Falling Time Cost of College: Evidence From Half a Century of Time Use Data," *Review of Economics and Statistics* 93, no. 2: 468–478.

6. National Center on Education and the Economy, "What Does It Really Mean to Be College and Work Ready?: The Mathematics and English Literacy Required of First Year Community College Students," http://www .ncee.org/college-and-work-ready/.

7. From 2001 to 2009, I was executive vice president of the Jack Kent Cooke Foundation, leading scholarship programs that worked directly with community college transfer students and grant programs aimed at developing partnerships between community colleges and eight highly selective four-year colleges to increase transfer opportunities for low-income and minority students.

8. Moreover, research reveals that, across higher education, efforts to improve teaching are hampered by inadequate access to learning outcomes information. For example, a 2010 study of regional accreditation found that "deficiencies in student learning outcomes assessment were the most common shortcoming in institutional evaluations." Staci Provezis, *Regional Accreditation and Student Learning Outcomes: Mapping the Territory,* Occasional Paper 6 (Champaign, IL: National Institute for Learning Outcomes Assessment, 2010), 7.

9. Community college developmental estimates come from Thomas Bailey, "Rethinking Developmental Education in Community College," CCRC Brief No. 40 (New York: Community College Research Center, Teachers

College, Columbia University, 2009). Bailey wrote that "it is reasonable to conclude that two thirds or more of community college students enter college with academic skills weak enough in at least one major subject area to threaten their ability to succeed in college-level courses." Four-year estimates come from the National Center for Education Statistics' *The Condition of Education* (Washington, DC: U.S. Department of Education, 2012). In 2007–2008, according to NCES, the portion of students who enrolled in at least one developmental course (which itself was far less than the portion with developmental needs) was 20 percent at four-year colleges and 42 percent at public two-year colleges.

10. This requirement came as part of West Kentucky's implementation of Six Sigma, a data-driven quality improvement process that originated in the business and manufacturing sectors.

11. The case for the use of coaching to improve instructor effectiveness is made convincingly by Atul Gawande in "Personal Best: Top Athletes and Singers Have Coaches. Should You?" *New Yorker*, October 3, 2011, http://www.newyorker.com/reporting/2011/10/03/111003fa_fact_gawande.

12. For more on the association's accreditation changes and focus on learning outcomes, see Rudolph S. Jackson et al., "Redesigning Regional Accreditation: The Impact on Institutional Planning," *Planning for Higher Education* 38, no. 4 (July–September 2010): 9–19.

13. For example, charter schools in the Uncommon Schools network have developed strong processes for assessing and improving teacher effectiveness based on student outcomes, led by principals who are trained as instructional leaders. For more information, see Paul Bambrick-Santoyo, *Driven by Data: A Practical Guide to Improve Instruction* (San Francisco: Jossey-Bass, 2012).

14. Kate Walsh and Christopher O. Tracy, *Increasing the Odds: How Good Policies Can Yield Better Teachers* (Washington, DC: National Council on Teacher Quality, 2004).

15. Scott E. Carrell and James E. West, "Does Professor Quality Matter? Evidence from Random Assignment of Students to Professors" (NBER Working Paper No. 14081, June 2008).

16. Peter Ewell, "Grading Student Learning: Better Luck Next Time," in *Measuring Up 2000: The State-by-State Report Card for Higher Education* (San Jose, CA: National Center on Public Policy and Higher Education, 2000).

17. *Measuring Up 2006: The State-by-State Report Card for Higher Education* (San Jose, CA: National Center on Public Policy and Higher Education, 2006).

<h3 style="text-align:center">CHAPTER 4</h3>

1. Aspen Institute College Excellence Program, *A Guide for Using Labor Market Data to Improve Student Success* (Washington, DC: Aspen Institute, 2013).
2. Complete College America, *Time Is the Enemy* (Washington, DC: Complete College America, 2011).
3. U.S. Department of Labor, Bureau of Labor Statistics, "Occupational Outlook Handbook 2012–2013 Edition, Radiation Therapists," http://www.bls .gov/ooh/healthcare/radiation-therapists.htm.
4. For this and more examples from three states, visit College Measures' Economic Success Metrics program at CollegeMeasures.org, "Economic Success Metrics (ESM) Program," www.collegemeasures.org/esm.
5. On differing completion rates, see Frederick Hess et al., *Diplomas and Dropouts: Which Colleges Actually Graduate Their Students (and Which Don't)* (Washington, DC: American Enterprise Institute, 2009). On choosing low-completion schools, see Melissa Roderick et al., *From High School to the Future: Potholes on the Road to College* (Chicago: University of Chicago Consortium on Chicago School Research, 2008), and William Bowen, Matthew M. Chingos, and Michael S. McPherson, *Crossing the Finish Line: Completing College at America's Public Universities* (Princeton, NJ: Princeton University Press, 2009).
6. Aspen Institute College Excellence Program, *A Guide for Using Labor Market Data*.
7. Ibid.
8. Response rates from graduates of programs about their employment and earnings have been reported to be as low as 6 percent. See Brad Fulton and Claire Porter, "State to Publish College Employment Rates," *Capital News Service*, May 16, 2012, http://capitalnews.vcu.edu/2012/05/16/ state-to-publish-college-grads-employment-rates/.
9. See, for example, Mark Schneider and Ben Vivari, *The Earnings Power of Graduates From Tennessee's Colleges and Universities: How Are Graduates from Different Degree Programs Doing in the Labor Market?* (Rockville, MD: College Measures, 2012). Many colleges simply don't provide labor market

data and graduate school enrollment outcomes data to prospective students at all, despite the requirements of the 2008 Higher Education Opportunity Act. See Kevin Carey and Andrew P. Kelly, *The Truth Behind Education Disclosure Laws* (Washington, DC: Education Sector, 2011).

10. A court decision makes it unclear whether these reports will be replicated in the future. Association of Private Colleges and Universities v. Arne Duncan, Secretary of the Department of Education, and United States Department of Education, 1:11-cv-00138 (United States Court of Appeals for the District of Columbia Circuit, 2012).

CHAPTER 5

1. Current data in this paragraph comes from Rahel Tekle, "Compensation and Benefits of Community College CEOs: 2012," *AACC Research Brief*, 2012, no. 2012-1. Presidency tenure from 1985 is from Kathryn M. Moore et al., *Today's Academic Leaders: A National Study of Administrators in Community and Junior Colleges* (University Park, PA: Center for the Study of Higher Education, Pennsylvania State University, 1984).

2. Tekle, "Compensation and Benefits"; Christopher Shults, "The Critical Impact of Impending Retirements on Community College Leadership," *AACC Research Brief*, 2001, no. 1.

3. In 2001, former community college president George Vaughan released an article discussing whether leadership turnover was a "crisis or opportunity." See George B. Vaughan, "Developing Community College Leaders for the Future: Crisis or Opportunity" (unpublished paper, ERIC, Document #ED 457-873, 2001).

4. A few states have released reports that detail the employment and earnings of students in every public college by every program. See Jon Marcus, "New Pressure on Colleges to Disclose Grads' Earnings," *The Hechinger Report*, January 16, 2013, http://hechingerreport.org/content/new-pressure-on-colleges-to-disclose-grads-earnings_10885/. Also, in the past four years, the U.S. Department of Education has for the first time automatically provided completion outcomes about individual colleges to student seeking financial aid; required that college Web sites present the net cost of completing a year of education; publicized earnings data, by program and institution, for graduates of thousands of technical and career programs; and drafted a consumer scorecard to show cost, graduation rates, and labor market outcomes for all colleges.

5. In 2010–2011, 7 percent of students at U.S. two-year colleges were enrolled in private for-profit schools. Laura G. Knapp, Janice E. Kelly-Reid, and Scott A. Ginder, *Postsecondary Institutions and Price of Attendance in 2011–12, Degrees and Other Awards Conferred: 2010–11, and 12-Month Enrollment: 2010–11: First Look (Provisional Data)*, NCES 2012-289rev (Washington, DC: U.S. Department of Education, National Center for Education Statistics, 2012).

6. In June 2013, the Aspen Institute and Achieving the Dream released a joint report, *Crisis and Opportunity: Aligning the Community College Presidency with Student Success.* Much of this chapter of the book is informed by my role as a researcher and coauthor of the report.

7. For the historical underpinnings of the institutional resistance to change at colleges, see Sanford Shugart, "The Challenge to Deep Change: A Brief Cultural History of Higher Education," *Planning for Higher Education* 41, no. 2 (2013).

8. Ibid.

9. See, for example, Center for Community College Student Engagement, *A Matter of Degrees: Promising Practices for Community College Student Success* (Austin: University of Texas at Austin, 2012).

10. Sanford Shugart, "Rethinking the College Completion Agenda: Principles That Move the Needle" (speech, Southern Association of Colleges and Schools Commission on Colleges, Dallas, TX, December 2012).

11. Charles Blaich and Kathy Wise, "Hampshire and Wabash Assessment Collaborative Reviews," Center of Inquiry in the Liberal Arts, Wabash College, http://www.liberalarts.wabash.edu/storage/Assessment_Collaborative_Review.pdf.

ACKNOWLEDGMENTS

I GREATLY APPRECIATE THE MANY PEOPLE who (and organizations that) made this book possible. Just because they are listed here doesn't mean they agree with what is written in these pages.

Linda Perlstein deserves immense credit not just for sharpening my written word, but also for lending her talents as an attentive interviewer, careful observer, and thoughtful critic of ideas and organization as I wrote. She also drafted some of the specific examples of exceptional practice in this book.

My sincere thanks to several researchers and practitioners who pushed my thinking and analysis in ways that informed the book's conclusions, including Elaine Baker, Anthony Carnevale, Robert Johnstone, Patrick Kelly, Sandy Shugart, Robert Templin, and Keith Witham, who also—along with Christian Arana—provided valuable research and editorial assistance. As importantly, I am indebted to those who led the implementation of the Aspen Prize process, especially Rachel Roth, Leo Fitzpatrick, and Kathy Booth. Last but certainly not least, the learning at the center of the book was made possible by the funders of the Aspen Prize for Community College Excellence and the New College Leadership Project: America Achieves, the Bank of America Charitable Foundation, Bloomberg Philanthropies, the Joyce Foundation, the JPMorgan Chase Foundation, the Kresge Foundation, Lumina Foundation, and the W. K. Kellogg Foundation.

ABOUT THE AUTHOR

JOSHUA S. WYNER is the founder and executive director of the Aspen Institute College Excellence Program, which aims to strengthen practice, policy, and leadership to substantially improve college student success. Among the initiatives Wyner established are the Aspen Prize for Community College Excellence, which recognizes schools that achieve outstanding student outcomes, and the New College Leadership Project, which seeks to align the recruitment, hiring, and professional development of college presidents with student success goals.

Before starting the Aspen program in 2011, Wyner spent the previous sixteen years working to improve educational outcomes and urban policy as a leader of nonprofit organizations, including the Jack Kent Cooke Foundation and DC Appleseed. He spent his early career as an organizer and policy analyst with Citizen Action, as a program evaluator at the U.S. Government Accountability Office, and as an environmental attorney. He lives with his wife and sons in Washington, DC.

INDEX